D0559529

what unites us

what unites us

★

written by Dan Rather
and Elliot Kirschner
art by Tim Foley

:01
First Second

NEW YORK

1

what is patriotism?

When I was a young boy, we didn't have much in the way of material possessions.
But around 1940 or '41, we got our first family car—a heavily used 1938 Oldsmobile that I can still see so clearly in my mind's eye.
It was a bit of a rolling wreck, but I didn't see it as anything but beautiful.
JH20

In my neighborhood, the notion of a ***family vacation*** was an unheard-of luxury.

Yet that year, as the ***Fourth of July*** approached, my mother had the idea of driving to the beach in Galveston to see the ***fireworks*** over the ***Gulf of Mexico***.

A trip from Houston to Galveston ***these days*** is relatively easy. At that time it was a ***big deal***.

I remember how hot the day was. The ***humidity*** must have been approaching 100 percent.

My mother had us sing ***patriotic songs***.

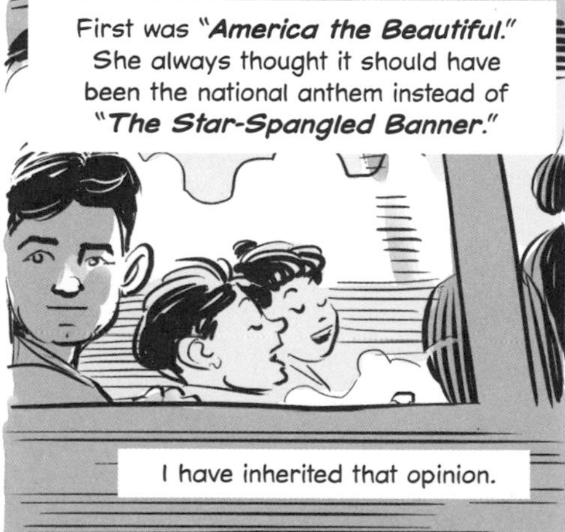
First was "***America the Beautiful***." She always thought it should have been the national anthem instead of "***The Star-Spangled Banner***."
I have inherited that opinion.

Deep in the heart of Texas . . .
I remember ***singing*** my heart out, and we ***repeated*** the songs ***over*** and ***over again***.

When we finally arrived in Galveston, it seemed *magical*.

We all sat on the *seawall* that had been built after the great hurricane of 1900.

We played on the *beach*, and when the sun went down—

—we watched the fireworks. In *retrospect* this was probably a *modest show*—low budget and low altitude—but I was *transfixed*.

I *knew*, after all, that *"the stars at night are big and bright deep in the heart of Texas."*

We had no money for the extravagances of a *hotel*, so the five of us slept in the car, curling up every which way.

I have often wished I could have *bottled* that day to taste its sweet innocence *once more*.

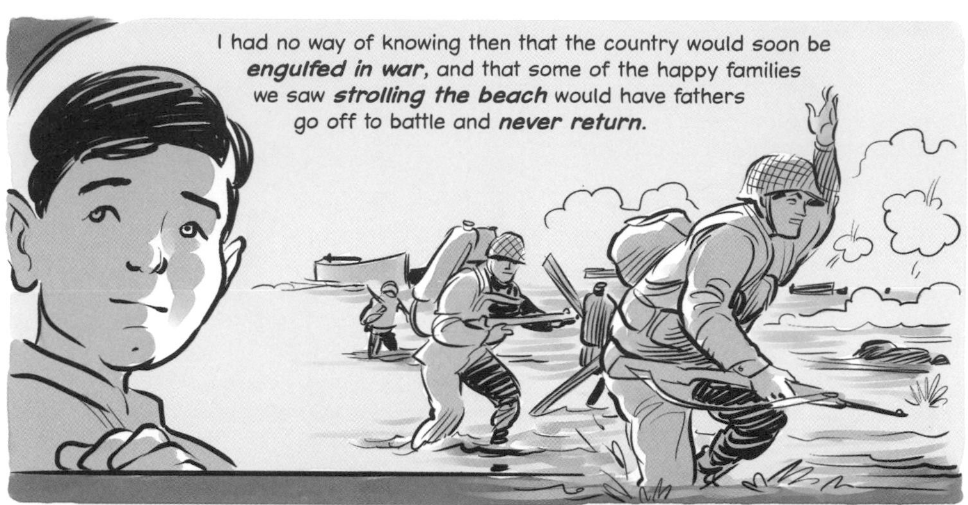
I had no way of knowing then that the country would soon be **engulfed in war,** and that some of the happy families we saw **strolling the beach** would have fathers go off to battle and **never return.**

I didn't know that I soon would be stricken by **rheumatic fever** and confined to my bed.

And I couldn't have anticipated that my **parents,** whom I can still picture sitting contentedly in the front seat, would **pass away** relatively early in my life.

All I knew then was that I liked the **feel of the road** and the sight of the scenery going past.
I liked going places...
...and I still do.

The ***open road*** has rightly become a symbol of America, a country whose ***destiny*** and ***people*** always seem to be ***on the move.***

And this family vacation helped fix an image of the ***United States*** in my mind as a land of wonder, awe, and optimism.

Who can say definitely ***when*** and ***how*** it begins, that first, faint sense of place, of ***belonging;*** that trickle that eventually becomes a ***wellspring*** of deep emotional ties to one's ***homeland?***

Childhood is often ***sentimentalized***, and I know now that the country I was growing to ***love*** had its ***flaws.*** I already knew the pain of the ***Great Depression*** and would soon live through the crisis of ***world war.***

I would then go on to a career that forced me to ***confront*** the often simmering and sometimes ***explosive injustices*** of the United States; its ***bigotry, exploitation, callousness***, and ***corruption***.

It may seem counterintuitive, but these ***flaws*** made me love my country ***even more.***

NO TO HATE
For I have seen how a nation can **pick itself up** and make progress, even at **divisive** and dysfunctional political moments like the **present** when we seem to be spinning **backward**.

I have found that the vast **majority** of men, women, and children I have met over the course of my life are **kind** and **well intentioned**.

For all the stories of **misdeeds** on which I have reported, there have been **many more** of **heroic actions** and communal **empathy**.

It is **true** that the news **headlines**—
DOOM
GLOOM
—often paint a **dark** and **dispiriting picture**.

5
But in every **community**, on every **day**, there are so **many** who choose to do the **right thing**.

Today we are a *divided* country.
Too many are being *told* that this nation is not for them, that their *values* make us *weaker*, that their *voice* is better left *unspoken*.
We see elected officials pounding their chests, saying their vision of America represents the only *real* patriotism.
To them I say that patriotism is *not a cudgel*.
It is not an *arms race*.
It means confronting honestly what is *wrong* or *sinful* with our *nation* and *government*.
DO NOT CROSS
I see my *love* of country imbued with a *responsibility* to bear witness to its *faults*.
It's *tragic* that those with the strongest ancestral tie to the land, the *Native Americans*, have so bitterly felt the *chasm* between the soaring words of our *Declaration of Independence* and *Constitution* and the harsh *reality* of governmental policy.

We are bound together by a *grand experiment* in government, the *rule of law*, and common bonds of *citizenship*. This is what it means to be an *American*.
But our creed has *long been* that all citizens can claim an equal legacy of this nation as their *own*, whether they *just* took the oath of *citizenship*, or have roots that *predate* the arrival of the *Mayflower*.
And we should neither forget nor be *paralyzed* by our prior *national sins*.
We must look *clear-eyed* at the problems of the past and present, but be encouraged that our *electoral* and *legal systems* provide a *framework* for improved justice in the *future*.
In his 1963 "*I Have a Dream*" speech during the March on Washington, *Dr. Martin Luther King Jr.* offered one of the most *eloquent* personal visions of *American patriotism* ever delivered.

"In a sense we've come to our nation's capital to ***cash a check.***

"When the architects of our republic wrote the magnificent words of the ***Constitution*** and the ***Declaration of Independence,*** they were signing a ***promissory note*** to which ***every*** American was to ***fall heir.***

"We ***refuse*** to ***believe*** that the bank of justice is ***bankrupt.*** We refuse to believe that there are ***insufficient funds*** in the great vaults of opportunity of this nation.

"So we've come to cash this check, a check that will give us ***upon demand*** the riches of ***freedom*** and the security of ***justice.***"

He wasn't arguing that there was something inherently ***rotten*** with the ***protections*** and ***provisions*** under which the United States was ***founded.***
Rather, he believed, and justly so, that the ***translation*** of those ideals into ***practice*** had been ***lacking.***
If our constitutional protections had been dispensed ***more equally*** and ***fairly,*** he asserted, then the ***dreams*** of which he spoke would be a lot closer to ***reality.***

MARCH
NOW!
MARCH
NOW!

In my years covering the ***civil rights movement***, I was always struck by the ***fierce determination*** of these men and women to fight for their place in the ***future*** of a country that had ***mistreated*** them.

They were infused with an ***unbreakable optimism*** that they would prevail. This spirit has echoed time and again by those who have demanded their full constitutional rights as ***American citizens***.

I have long been suspicious of those who would vociferously and publicly bestow the title of "***patriot***" upon themselves with an ***air*** of ***superiority***.

And I have generally taken a skeptical view of those who are ***quick*** to ***pass judgment*** on the depths of patriotism in ***others***.

George Washington warned future generations *"to guard against the impostures of pretended patriotism."*

An admonition, not ***only*** to be wary of the ***patriotic posturing*** of others—

—but also to be alert to the stirrings of pretended patriotism within ***oneself***.

It is important not to confuse "***patriotism***" with "***nationalism.***"

As I define it, "***nationalism***" is a ***monologue*** in which you place your country in a position of ***moral*** and ***cultural supremacy*** over others.

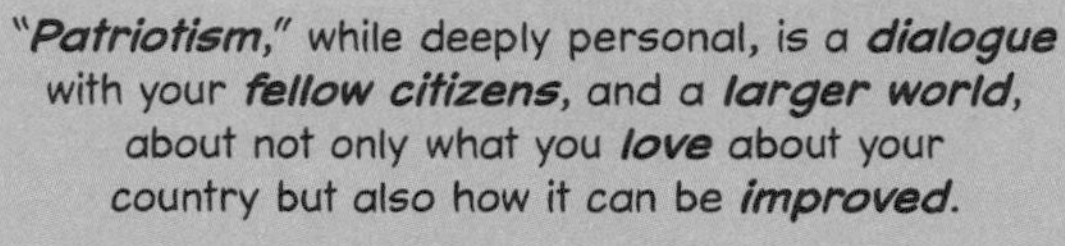
"***Patriotism,***" while deeply personal, is a ***dialogue*** with your ***fellow citizens,*** and a ***larger world,*** about not only what you ***love*** about your country but also how it can be ***improved.***

Patriotism is rooted in ***humility.***
Nationalism is rooted in ***arrogance.***

Unchecked ***nationalism*** leads to ***conflict and war.*** Unbridled ***patriotism*** can lead to the ***betterment*** of society.

The descent from patriotism to nationalism can be subtle and ***dangerous,*** and I am reminded of those weeks and months after the terror attacks of ***September 11, 2001.***

We wavered amid a climate of ***panic*** and ***hubris.***

We limited our ***civil liberties*** (the Patriot Act), undermined our ***moral traditions*** (torture), and ultimately launched a ***bloody*** and ***costly*** foreign misadventure (Iraq).

Dissent, the rule of law, and deliberations on acts of war are all ***hallmarks*** of the best ideals of ***American patriotism,*** but they were marginalized during a fervor of ***nationalism.***

The *flag pin* was
a potent symbol
of that era.

In 2007, presidential
candidate ***Barack
Obama*** created a ***stir***
when he ***declined*** to
wear a flag pin.

He explained:
Shortly after 9/11,
the flag pin became a
substitute for, I think,
true patriotism,
which is speaking out
on issues that are of
importance to our
national security.

Patriotism—
active, constructive
patriotism—
takes ***work.***

It takes ***knowledge,
engagement*** with those
who are different from
you, and ***fairness*** in
law and opportunity.

It takes coming together
for ***good causes.***
This is one of the things
I cherish ***most*** about
the United States:

We are a nation not
only of dreamers,
but also ***fixers.***

Like so many, I love my ***country*** and its ***people.***
I do so with a ***sentimentality*** that may seem anachronistic in today's more ***jaded*** world.
Our nation will not ***survive*** as we know it without an ***engaged*** and ***committed*** population.
"***We the people,***" all of us, are living together in perhaps the greatest ***social*** and governmental ***experiment*** ever ***conceived.***
We are being ***tested.***

How can we ***prepare*** ourselves for this moment?
Are we up to the ***challenge***?

2

freedom

the vote
I would like to be able to say that I came out of the womb with a deep sense of fairness, but it would not be true.
The truth is, for most of my early life, I had too little consciousness about race, and I didn't have any deep personal empathy.
It was just a fact.
The banality of racism and segregation was one of its most disturbing qualities.
There is one moment from my youth, however, that is seared in my mind.

I was in my ***early teens,*** and my father decided it was time I attend a ***precinct meeting*** to learn about ***civic life.***
HALL

The way politics in most states worked back then was that candidates were selected at ***state*** and ***national*** party conventions, not ***primaries.***

A precinct meeting chose delegates for a ***county convention,*** which selected ***delegates*** for the state or national ***party gatherings.***

In ***Texas*** in the 1940s, being a ***Democratic candidate*** was tantamount to election, just as it had been since the ***Civil War.***

If you want to see a ***Republican,*** I'll take you to the ***Hermann Park zoo.*** I hear they got one stuffed there.

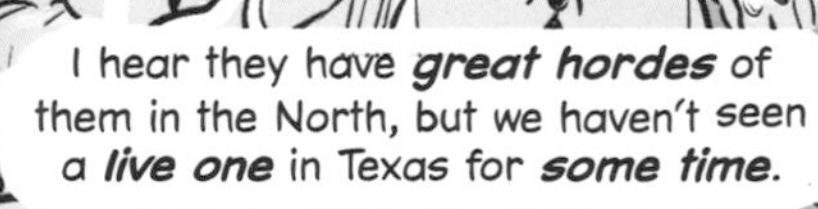
I hear they have ***great hordes*** of them in the North, but we haven't seen a ***live one*** in Texas for ***some time.***

Precinct meetings were often ***raucous affairs,*** sort of like the ***old party conventions*** you see in historical documentaries—
—a ***far cry*** from the scripted events of ***today.***

Attendance at these meetings was normally an all-white affair. But that night, the first such event I had attended, was different.

There were four or five ***African American*** men also in attendance. By ***law***, they had every right to be there. It was their precinct, too, as my neighborhood, the ***Heights***, abutted a predominantly African American neighborhood. But ***law*** and ***custom*** can be very different things.

Dad, what's ***happening?***
I'll explain later.

When ***they*** get up, ***we*** get up.
All those who ***support*** the measure, ***rise***.

I'm ***not*** suggesting my father was a ***hero***.

For his time and place, he was ***remarkably*** unprejudiced.

But he was ***not*** a trailblazer.

His rationale in this case was ***straightforward***: These men had fought in the ***war*** and they were ***entitled*** to vote.

It was just a matter of ***fairness***.

But it didn't fully register. I noted it and apparently filed it away for a time when I was more prepared to understand its lessons.
HALL

When I joined CBS News in 1962, I got myself assigned to the civil rights beat.
CBS NEWS

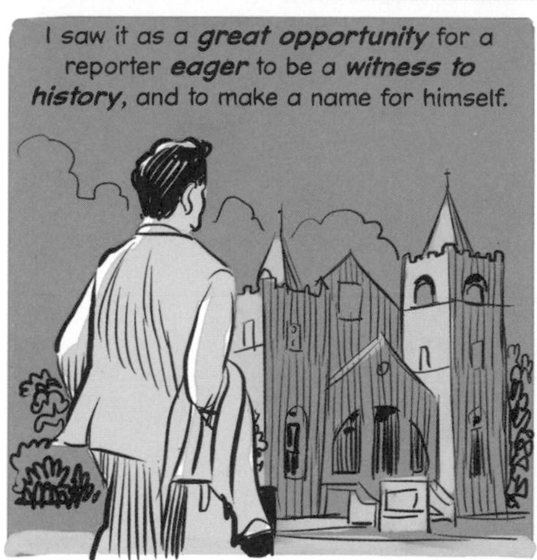
I saw it as a great opportunity for a reporter eager to be a witness to history, and to make a name for himself.

One of my first stops—
—was meeting Dr. Martin Luther King Jr. in Albany, Georgia.

Being in the room with King, hearing him praise Mahatma Gandhi and nonviolent protest, sensing his deep spirituality based on both his Christian faith and his readings of philosophy—
—all of this started to focus me.

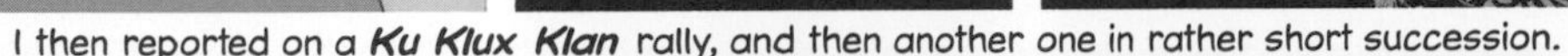
I then reported on a ***Ku Klux Klan*** rally, and then another one in rather short succession.

Suddenly the ***stakes*** of the movement were ***very*** apparent.

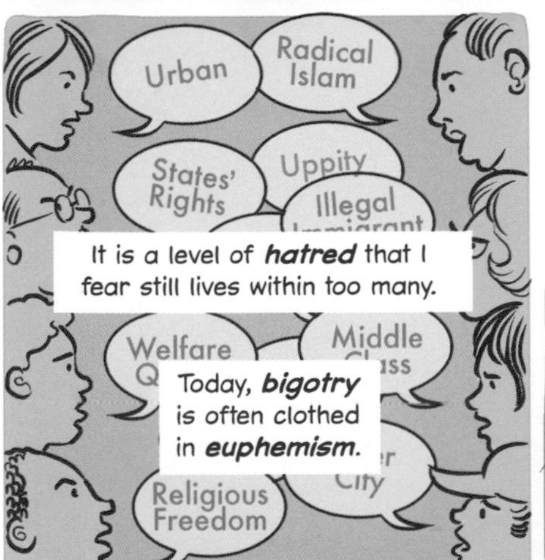
Urban
Radical Islam
States' Rights
Uppity
Illegal
It is a level of ***hatred*** that I fear still lives within too many.
Welfare
Middle
Today, ***bigotry*** is often clothed in ***euphemism***.
Religious Freedom

I headed to ***Jackson, Mississippi***. I walked the streets, asked whom should I talk to.
I needed to meet Mr. Evers. Medgar Evers.

While other leaders, such as King, sought a ***broad mandate*** of social change on a ***variety*** of issues—including, of course, the ***right to vote***—
—Evers was ***different***.
He was ***focused*** like a ***laser beam*** on voting.

What proceeded was a simple morality play, but one that shaped me as much or more than almost any other event in my lifetime.
What are you doing here, boy?
I've come with these fine people to vote.
We have all the proper papers and are registered.
Well, I'm telling you—
—they ain't gonna vote!

Suddenly everything snapped to attention in my mind.
VOTE
TOD
I retroactively understood the deep sin of segregation and racism that had enveloped me my entire life.

To write this now is to be shocked anew by my *naivete* and *blindness*. I wish I had seen all of this *earlier*.

But the brazenness of a white election official tossing aside the constitutional right of enfranchisement—
VOT
—a right that entered the Constitution only after the Civil War, our bloodiest conflict, made me seethe with anger.

I do remember ***sharing*** my ***experience*** later with my ***soundman***, who was from ***Alabama***.

What did you ***expect*** to happen?

Not ***that***.

Well, that's how it is in a ***lot*** of places...

I knew what I was ***seeing*** and I was determined to bring this story into ***living rooms*** across the ***nation***.

There was a ***disconnect*** back then between what was happening in the ***South*** and what the ***rest*** of the nation knew.

This was ***not America*** as I had envisioned it. And I wanted my countrymen and women to ***know*** this, too.

I felt a great ***certainty*** in the separation of ***right*** from ***wrong***.
My relationship with my country would ***never*** be the ***same***.

Patriotism would require ***standing up*** to what I had ***seen***—
—not standing alongside it in ***silence***.

I witnessed in Medgar Evers that day the very definition of courage and love of country—
—his country, my country, our country.

After that moment, Evers and I spent more time together.

Remarkably, I found very little hatred in the man.

He hated the system and the elected officials who manipulated it.
He saw most of his white neighbors as decent Christian people who were just horribly misguided on race.

However, I had a sense from that first reporting trip that Evers was living on borrowed time.

To stand up for the right to vote was to challenge all the power of the Southern status quo.

I was in Tuscaloosa, Alabama, in *June of 1963*, when we got the *call*. It came from King's headquarters.

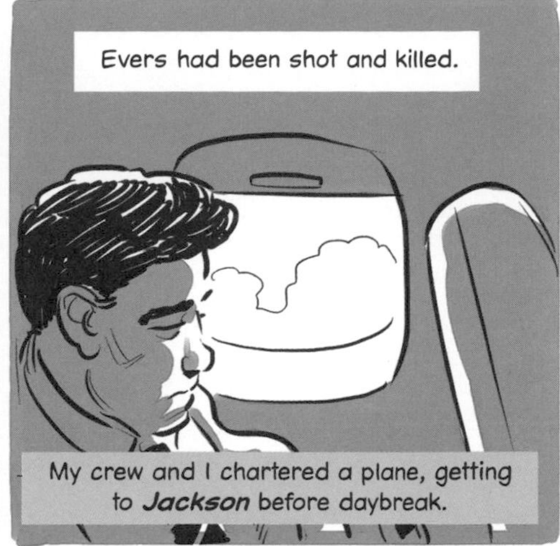
Evers had been shot and killed.
My crew and I chartered a plane, getting to *Jackson* before daybreak.

It was a calculated and *cold-blooded* assassination.

African Americans' feelings ranged from *outrage* to despondency.
But there was also a deep resolve to *persist*.

Among white people, a fair number felt Evers had gotten what he *deserved*.
Most wanted to go on as if *nothing* had happened.
There *might* have been those who felt it was *terrible* and we needed to *change* our ways.
But *I* didn't find them.

So many of our problems today are ***directly linked*** to the way we vote or how we are subtly ***prohibited*** from voting.

In some ways, we have worked hard to ***enhance*** the ease of casting a ballot; we have ***early voting*** and ***voting by mail*** in many states.
But we see today ***echoes*** of the century after the ***Civil War***, when African Americans had the ***right*** to vote by ***law***—
VOTE
TODAY
—but ***not*** always in practice.

Back then, local politicians invented ***arbitrary tests*** and other barriers to limit access to the vote.
REGISTRAR
LITERACY
TEST
TODAY
Today, these voter suppression efforts still often ***target*** the most marginal members of society.
VOTE
VOTE
YES
ON B

It is easier for a ***white-collar worker*** to alter his or her schedule to vote,
BUS
STOP
but for a ***single mother*** punching a clock...

VOTING
PRECINCT 5

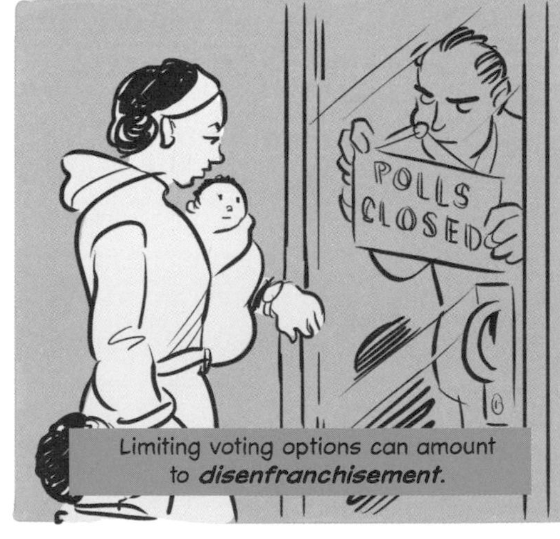
POLLS
CLOSED
Limiting voting options can amount to ***disenfranchisement***.

It is one of the **great** truisms of a democratic form of government: that not only **political power** but the very **definition of citizenship** is predicated on the **right to vote.**

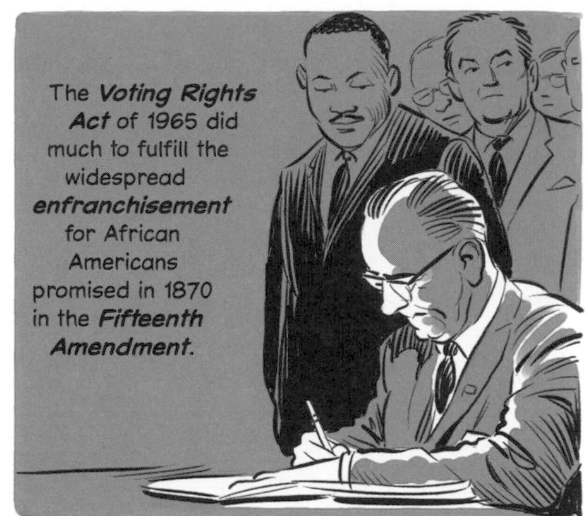
The **Voting Rights Act** of 1965 did much to fulfill the widespread **enfranchisement** for African Americans promised in 1870 in the **Fifteenth Amendment.**

But a recent **Supreme Court ruling** has removed **key provisions** of the Voting Rights Act, and many of the **gains** we've seen are being **curtailed** under specious claims of **voter fraud.**

So we see states passing **voter ID laws** and other hurdles, even though the **truth** is that in-person voter fraud is so rare as to be **statistically nonexistent.**
PROOF OF
CITIZENSHI

The **real danger** to the sanctity of the vote lies in **suppression.**

It is *inevitable* that the battle lines of the recent *voting wars* have centered on *race.*
Indeed, these narratives—*race* and *voting*—are inextricably *intertwined.*

Those who seek to *suppress voting* today are either *ignorant* of the history, or are, as I *suspect* is more often the case, *malevolently* choosing to ignore it.

To suppress the vote is to make a *mockery* of democracy.
Those who *do* are essentially *admitting* that their policies are *unpopular.*

If you can't convince a *majority* of voters that your ideas are *worthy*, you try to *limit* the pool of voters.

This reveals a certain irony:

Many who are *most vocal* in championing a free, open, and dynamic economy are the *same political factions* that suppress these principles when it comes to the *currency* of *ideas.*

And there are many ways to suppress and distort the vote.

Gerrymandering isn't just a *recent* phenomenon.

The word was coined in 1812 when Massachusetts governor *Elbridge Gerry* went to such egregious lengths to *redraw* the state senate districts in his party's *favor*—

—that one district took on the shape of a *salamander*.

More *recently*, gerrymandering has been taken to a *new extreme*,
and *neither* of the major political parties is *entirely blameless*.

Aided by *powerful* computer data analysis—
—it is now *possible* to draw district lines—

—in such a way as to swing considerably—
—the balance of state *legislative* and *congressional* delegations.

Gerrymandering is *now* often used to *stifle* minority representation by congregating voters in *districts* to lessen their overall *political power*—
—and some of the fiercest *court battles* on *voting* are taking place in this arena.
SMITH FOR MAYOR
VOTE J
VOTE JONES
A *shrinking* and *polarized* electorate *damages* our democracy.
Removing the very *competition* for votes that is at the *heart* of our democracy.
It lessens *enthusiasm* and civic engagement, which leads to *apathy*.

One can actively ***suppress*** votes or make voting seem ***meaningless***. They are ***two paths*** to the ***same destination***.

Our voting participation is ***far below*** the levels of a ***healthy*** democracy.
That ***should*** worry all of us.

In that neighborhood precinct meeting many decades ago, I saw democracy as an ***activity*** and a ***civic duty***.

I saw the ***same thing*** in the determination of ***Medgar Evers*** and his followers.

It is an act of ***speech,*** a ***demand*** that your voice be heard, that you are included in the ***republic.***
Lessening this bond of citizenship, either ***forcibly*** or through ***indifference,*** makes us less free and less resilient as a nation.

dissent

We may *live* in a democracy of *majority* rule,

but one of our most *important* founding *ideals* was to confer legal protection on those *unafraid* to *buck* popular sentiment with *contrarian voices.*

NO!

Dissent can sometimes be uncomfortable, but it is ***vital*** in a democracy.

Dissent is doubly ***necessary*** to resist a slide into greater ***autocracy.***

That is why our *First Amendment* is so *important.*
We the People
Free speech must be protected so that we can hear from those who *challenge* our beliefs.

And a *free* and *independent press* is *essential* for bringing *dissenting opinions* to the national conversation.

My ***first inklings*** of the importance of dissent came during the ***anti-communist witch hunts*** of the early 1950s—
—epitomized by the ***reign of terror*** under Wisconsin senator ***Joseph McCarthy.***

Before McCarthy, there was ***Martin Dies Jr.***
He was a ***classic demagogue*** who railed against a federal government ***riddled with:***
Hundreds of left-wingers and ***radicals*** who do not believe in our system of ***private enterprise.***

In 1952, the ***Minute Women*** and other like-minded groups put forward a slate of ***ardent anti-communists*** for the school board in my hometown of Houston, Texas—
—setting up a showdown with ***moderates*** on the ballot.
BETTER DEAD THAN RED

After **college** and a short stint in the Marines, I got a brief tryout to work at the **Houston Chronicle** in 1954 under the editorship of **Martin Emmet Walter**, a strident **anti-communist**.

ON AIR
KTRH
I didn't last long at the newspaper (too poor at spelling, for one thing), but the **Chronicle** moved me over to the **radio station** the paper owned, and we started doing **daily reports** from the city desk in the paper's **newsroom**.

It was there that I got a wonderful mentor in an editor named **Dan Cobb**, the first dissenter I ever got to know.

He had no **tolerance** for the malignancy of the **Red Scare**.
He would provide quiet but encouraging **counsel**.

I know you are **worried**, but we have to **outlast** this.
We must work within the **confines** of the **possible**; it is our job to report the news as **straight** as we can.

One evening I was reporting ***live*** on the ***radio*** from the newspaper's city desk on a round of contentious ***school board elections*** when some results came in that were ***bad*** for a slate of anti-communist candidates on the ballot.

I made some ***mention*** of it on the air, not knowing that ***Walter*** was behind me.
KTRH

This young man doesn't know what he's talking about!
KTRH

KTRH

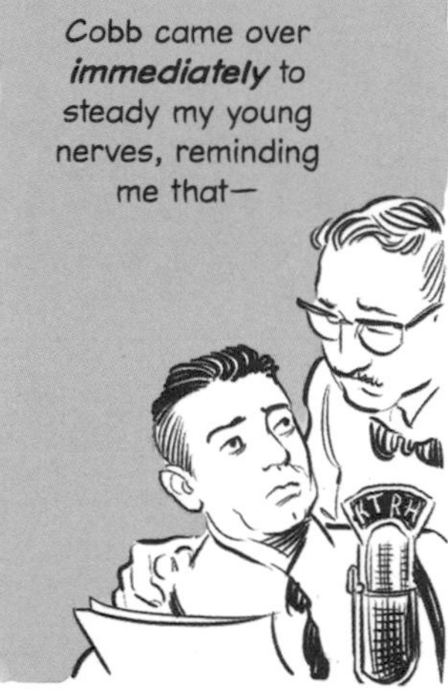

Cobb came over ***immediately*** to steady my young nerves, reminding me that—
KTRH

As a ***reporter***, it is your job to ***tell it*** as you ***see it***.
KTRH

It is that ***age-old dilemma:***

Do you ***stay*** and try to ***change*** the church from ***within***, or ***leave*** the church?

Oftentimes, Walter would want a straight news story ***rewritten*** to give it his ***preferred*** slant—

—but ***Cobb*** would go ahead and publish the ***original***, claiming he was on a deadline.
It was a subtle form of dissent, but it was ***effective***.

The drama playing out at the *Chronicle* ***paled in comparison*** to the dangers posed to the nation ***at large.*** Over the course of just a few years, ***thousands*** of lives were ***broken*** by lost jobs and ***shattered reputations.*** Some of the victims were famous—

—like those on the ***Hollywood Blacklist.***
Most, however, were ***everyday people.***
One of the lessons of the Red Scare is that the long arc of history often ***validates*** the ***dissenters,*** a striking example being the ***Vietnam War.***
Today it is largely acknowledged to have been a tragic ***mistake,*** but when I first went to cover the war in ***1965–66***—
—the conflict and the anti-communist impulses that ***fueled it*** were still largely ***popular*** across the ***political spectrum***—
THAILAND
BANGKOK
CAMBODIA
SOUTH VIETNAM
—but ***especially*** with politicians in Washington.

There were **some** dissenting voices on **Vietnam** from the beginning, but they tended to be on the **far end** of the political **left**.

Mark Hatfield, a moderate Republican governor from Oregon, was a **notable exception**.

Another dissenter of note was Minnesota senator **Eugene McCarthy**, who broke with **President Lyndon Johnson**, a fellow **Democrat**, over the war.

After the North Vietnamese and the Vietcong launched the **Tet Offensive** in January of 1968, popular opinion further shifted **against** the war.

I shall **not** seek, and I will **not accept**, the nomination of my party for **another term** as your president.
Dissent is **most controversial** during wartime because it is cast as **unpatriotic** and **dangerous** to the **national cause**.
But that is **precisely** the time when a democracy should be asking itself **difficult** and **uncomfortable** questions.

Jeannette Rankin, a fierce critic of the Vietnam War, had a long history of political activism.
In 1917, she was one of only fifty representatives to vote against American entry in World War I.
As a woman, I can't go to war, and I refuse to send anyone else.

I feel we are a better and stronger nation for having such voices.

The role of dissent is to force all of us to question our dogmas and biases.

In the same vein, on April 4, 1967, Dr. Martin Luther King Jr. took the pulpit at Riverside Church in New York for one of the most consequential and controversial speeches of his career.
It was entitled "Beyond Vietnam: A Time to Break the Silence."
WRVR

Instead of the optimism of "I Have a Dream," there was a weariness verging on pessimism.
We as a nation must undergo a radical revolution of values.

At the time, many commentators and even some of King's allies said that the civil rights leader should have kept his focus on ***racial justice*** instead of the ***war***.

I figure I was ***politically*** unwise, but ***morally*** wise.
I think I have a role to play which may be ***unpopular***.
That ***quote*** is as elegant a definition of ***dissent*** as you are likely to find.

In all the sanitized reimaginings of King's legacy, the Riverside Church speech is too often ***forgotten***.
That is a mistake because it captures both the complexities of the times and of a man who was one of the ***great dissenters*** in American history.

Fighting for ***justice*** is ***rarely*** smooth—
—and dissent requires ***steely resolve***.

I think the ***answer*** lies in the nature of principled dissent.
We have a ***long history*** in the United States of ***marginalized*** voices eventually convincing majorities through the ***strength*** of their ***ideas***.
Our democratic machinery provides ***fertile soil*** where seeds of change can ***grow***.
Few knew that ***better*** than ***King***.

NO!
While some dissenters are *famous,* most act on much smaller stages.
But that does *not* mean their actions are *any less courageous.*

To *stand up* and say something isn't right takes *guts,* no matter *who* you are, but it is especially true for *those* who have traditionally been—

—more *vulnerable* members of society.

Dissenters are not always *right.*

They are certainly not *all* people one would *admire,* and sometimes their *motives* are complicated or *unknowable.*

It is *messy.*
It is *controversial.*
WikiLeaks

But it is *often* consequential.
NO!

The United States was born from perhaps one of the **most radical** lines of dissenting speech in human history—
IN CONGRESS, JULY 4 1776
—the idea that the citizens of a land should live by the **consent** of the **governed** and **not** the whims of a **monarch.**

Dwight D. Eisenhower famously paid homage to this history in a **1954 speech** during the height of the Red Scare:
Here in America we are descended in blood and in spirit from **revolutionaries** and **rebels**— men and women who dared to **dissent** from accepted doctrine.
As their **heirs,** may we never confuse honest dissent with **disloyal subversion.**

This is especially true at the **Supreme Court,** where many of the most **famous** dissents have **pointed the way** for the future direction of the country.

Back in 1896 in *Plessy v. Ferguson*—
—the one dissenter was ***Justice John Marshall Harlan,*** who ***famously admonished*** his fellow jurists and the ***nation as a whole.***

*Our Constitution is **color-blind,** and neither knows nor tolerates classes among citizens.*
*In respect of **civil rights,** all citizens are **equal** before the law.*
*The **humblest** is the peer of the most **powerful.***

US MARSHAL
US MARSHA
More than half a century later, the Supreme Court would ***validate*** Harlan's humanity with a ***unanimous decision*** in *Brown v. Board of Education.*

In World War I, Congress passed an **Espionage Act** and a **Sedition Act**.
Used to prosecute and **imprison** men and women for their **speech**—
—including the famous socialist leader **Eugene Debs**.

And yet out of this period of restriction came one of the most **stirring** articulations of the **importance** of dissent in American history.
Fittingly, and perhaps **poetically**, it came in an **actual legal dissent**.

Abrams v. United States (1919) involved a group of Russian immigrants who had distributed pamphlets advocating **against** the **war effort**.

The Supreme Court had **twice ruled** unanimously to uphold the constitutionality of congressional acts to **stifle dissent**.

In both cases, the opinion was written by **Justice Oliver Wendell Holmes**.
He was **later** beset by friends and legal scholars who felt he had gone **too far** in suppressing speech.

When the decision came down in *Abrams*, the convictions were **upheld**, but it was **not** unanimous.
Two justices dissented, including **Holmes**.

Holmes had come to his decision by *listening* to others who had disagreed with him.

His dissent was, *therefore,* a product of *dissent*.

The ultimate *good* desired is better reached by *free trade* in ideas...
The best test of *truth* is the power of the thought to get itself *accepted* in the competition of the *market*,

and that truth is the *only ground* upon which their wishes safely can be *carried out*.
I think we should be eternally *vigilant* against attempts to check the expression of *opinions* that we loathe...

unless they so imminently *threaten* immediate interference with the lawful and pressing purposes of the *law* and that an immediate check is required to *save the country*.
NO!

NO!

NO!
NO!
NO!
NO!
America works best when
new thoughts can emerge
to compete, and thrive,
in a marketplace of ideas.

the press

In his novel *1984*, ***George Orwell*** laid out a ***dystopian vision*** of a world where words cease to have ***meaning***—

—history is continually ***rewritten***, and the notion of ***truth*** is forever lost.

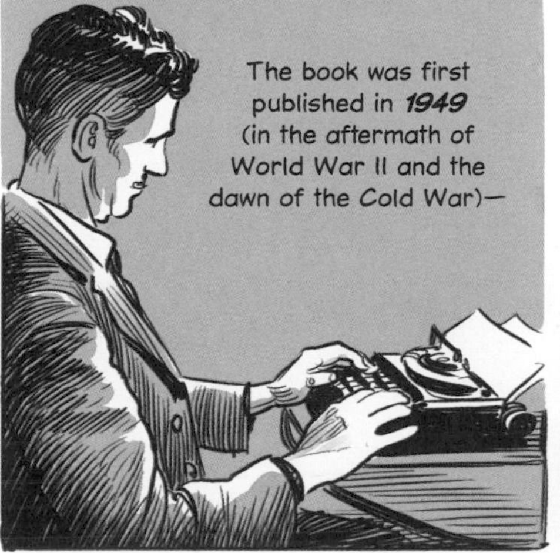
The book was first published in 1949 (in the aftermath of World War II and the dawn of the Cold War)—

—but its exploration of a society in which propaganda is the only currency of communication is resonant once more.

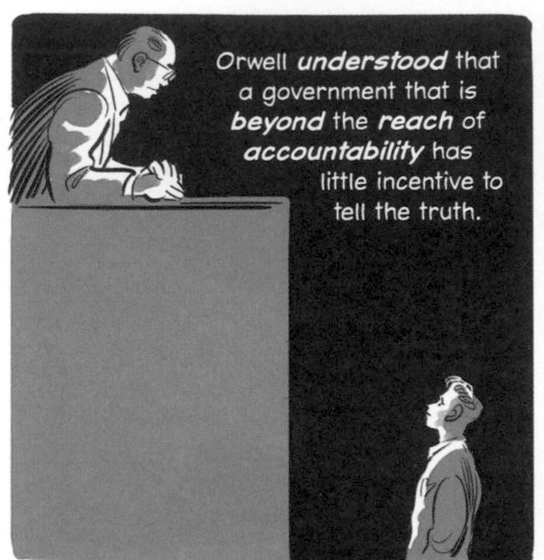
Orwell ***understood*** that a government that is ***beyond*** the ***reach*** of ***accountability*** has little incentive to tell the truth.

Indeed, its ***power*** may arise from the ***obliteration*** of objective ***facts.***
CHOCOLATE RATION
UNPERSON

In the world of *1984,* ***contradictory statements*** lose all sense of ***context*** and we are left with ***preposterous slogans:***
WAR IS PEACE
FREEDOM IS SLAVE
IGNORANCE IS STRENGTH

And yet Orwell asks us, if there is no one with the ***power*** to call a ***lie*** a ***lie,*** does it end up ***ceasing*** to be a ***lie?***

Our ***Founding Fathers***, after breaking free from monarchical subjugation, were ***determined to construct*** a government of ***checks*** and ***balances*** on absolute concentrated power.

So they created a ***federal system*** with differentiations between ***state*** and ***national*** control—

—as well as ***three branches*** of government—
EXECUTIVE
—that had to answer to ***one another***.
—with distinct ***powers*** and ***responsibilities***—
LEGISLATIVE
JUDICIAL

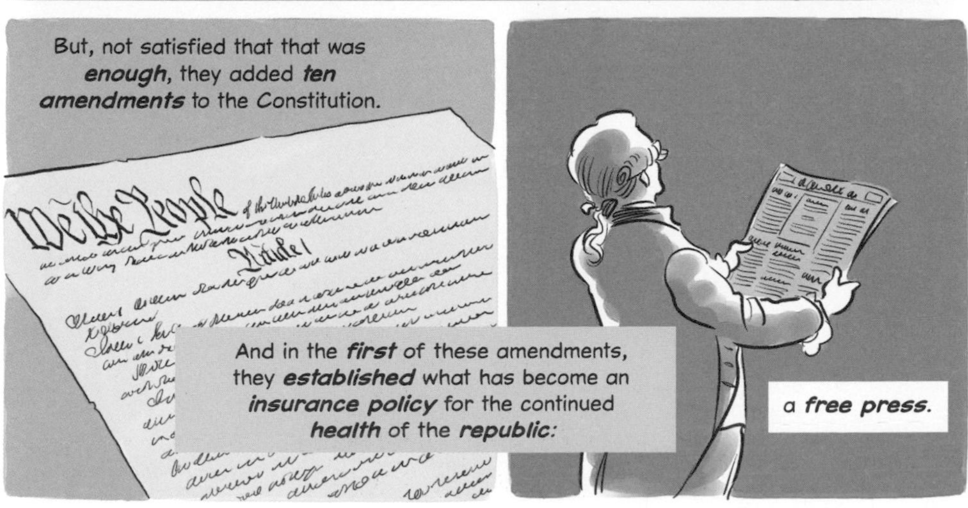
But, not satisfied that that was ***enough***, they added ***ten amendments*** to the Constitution.
We the People
And in the ***first*** of these amendments, they ***established*** what has become an ***insurance policy*** for the continued ***health*** of the ***republic:***
a ***free press***.

The role of the press is to ***ask hard questions*** and refuse to be deterred even when someone ***powerful*** claims:

Nothing to see ***here.***

At ***first glance,*** it might seem as if the press is a ***destabilizing force:***
It can ***undermine*** the ***credibility*** of our elected officials and ***ultimately*** our confidence in government.

It can drive down ***stock prices*** and ***embolden*** our nation's ***critics*** and ***enemies.***

It can uncover ***inconvenient*** truths—

—and stir ***divisions*** within our society.

But our Founding Fathers ***understood*** that long-term accountability—

—is ***more important*** than short-term stability.

Where would America be without the dogged work of the Boston Globe in documenting sexual abuse within the Catholic Church?
Boston Sunday Globe
Church allowed abuse by priest for years
US comes up empty in search for Omar
Antitrust exception shields baseball
Because of the press, powerful institutions are held accountable for their actions, and we become a stronger nation.
Press
Presently, the institution of a free press in America is in a state of crisis greater than I have ever seen in my lifetime—
—and perhaps in any moment in this nation's history.
Sustained attacks on press freedom from those in political power—
—rapidly changing technologies—
—crumbling business models—
—and some self-inflicted wounds.

Of course there has always been friction between those in power and the journalists tasked with covering them.

But as a public official in the United States—
—you agree to subject yourself and your actions to scrutiny.

The presidency of Richard Nixon was different and became an inflection point in the history of the free press in the United States.
He attacked the press, disengaged from them, and instituted a strategy of sidelining national media outlets in favor of staged events and interviews with local reporters—

—reporters who, in what would likely be their one and only interview with a president, were less willing to ask hard questions.

And it is not an accident that one of the architects of this strategy was a young Roger Ailes,
who would advise future Republican presidents and then monetize the demonization of a supposedly "biased" press by creating Fox News.

Ailes ***understood*** that there were ***long-simmering currents*** among millions of Americans—
—who felt ***persecuted*** by liberal elites and by extension the ***national press*** headquartered in places like ***New York.***

This antagonism was not ***theoretical*** and could be ***violent.***

Senator Joseph McCarthy tarred journalists during the ***communist witch hunts.***

But ***Nixon*** was the first to do it on the ***national level***—
—and ***win*** the presidency.

None of us could have predicted how ***technological*** and ***regulatory changes*** would usher in a ***new media landscape*** that, building on the Nixon legacy, would ***transform*** the very nature of news.

In ***1987***, under ***President Ronald Reagan,*** the Federal Communications Commission (FCC) abolished the ***Fairness Doctrine.***

In place since 1949, it had stipulated ***equal airtime*** for differing points of view.

In this environment where media outlets felt ***less compelled*** to present balanced political ***debate,*** AM radio stations in particular started to switch to a ***lucrative*** form of programming—
—best exemplified by ***Rush Limbaugh***—right-wing talk radio.

In the 1980s and 1990s the advent of ***cable television*** broadened what had been a ***limited*** number of stations—
CNN
TBS
FOX
—into a ***diverse*** lineup of ***niche networks.***

Into this business opportunity stepped ***Fox News*** and ***Mr. Ailes.***

Fox specializes in broadcasting opinion rather than news, and this opinion is often in service of ***conservative*** political objectives ***regardless*** of the facts.

More recently, the entire journalism business model has been upended by the rise of the Internet—
—and, even more recently, social media.
Suddenly anyone can be a news publisher, regardless of their expertise, sense of fairness, or motives.
And "fake news" from individual or state actors can spread like wildfire through Facebook, Twitter, and other similar outlets.

I do not think attacks on the American press as ***biased*** hold up to ***scrutiny.***

Reporters by their nature tend to be suspicious, especially of ***accrued power,*** and that usually extends to ***political parties.***

The effects of the ***sustained attacks*** on the press from ***politicians*** and ***coordinated media campaigns*** have been cumulative, ***intimidating reporters***—and, more important, editors, publishers, and owners—in newsrooms ***across the country.***

Despite the ***negative perception*** in some circles, almost every ***American journalist*** I have ever met is, at their ***core,*** patriotic.

These days, I fear that the pull of our inborn patriotism combined with a fear of being labeled un-American clouds that role—
—with real and potentially corrosive effects.

These are forces every journalist must be aware of, and on guard against.
But often our individual defenses fail, and sometimes they fail en masse with disastrous consequences.

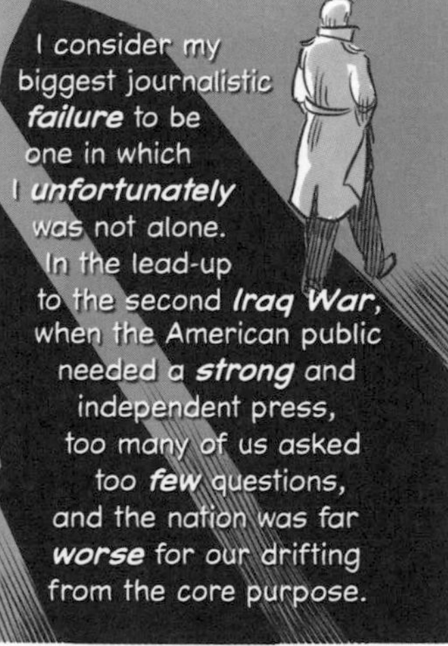
I consider my biggest journalistic failure to be one in which I unfortunately was not alone. In the lead-up to the second Iraq War, when the American public needed a strong and independent press, too many of us asked too few questions, and the nation was far worse for our drifting from the core purpose.

On the morning of September 11, 2001, as I rushed to the CBS News broadcast studio, I could see the columns of smoke rising amid a brilliant blue sky.

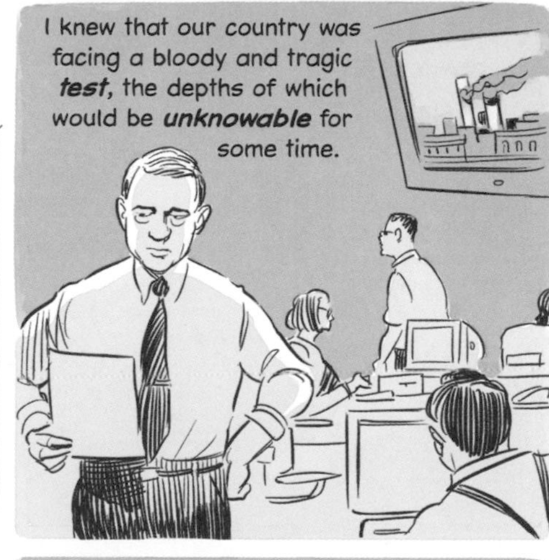
I knew that our country was facing a bloody and tragic test, the depths of which would be unknowable for some time.

It is easy to forget what those days, weeks, and months that followed felt like.

The immediate task in newsrooms like ours was to make sense of the moment.
"Al-Qaeda" became a household word, and there was palpable fear that another large-scale attack was imminent.

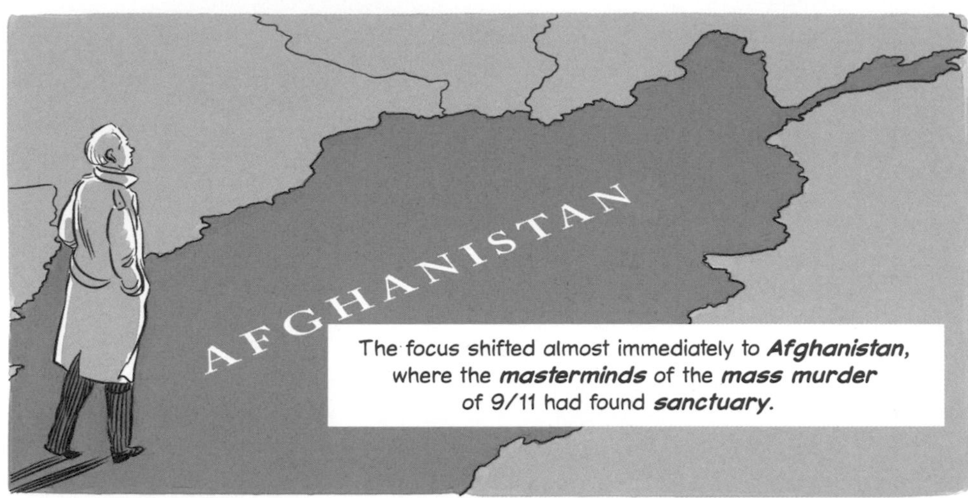
AFGHANISTAN
The focus shifted almost immediately to ***Afghanistan***, where the ***masterminds*** of the ***mass murder*** of 9/11 had found ***sanctuary***.

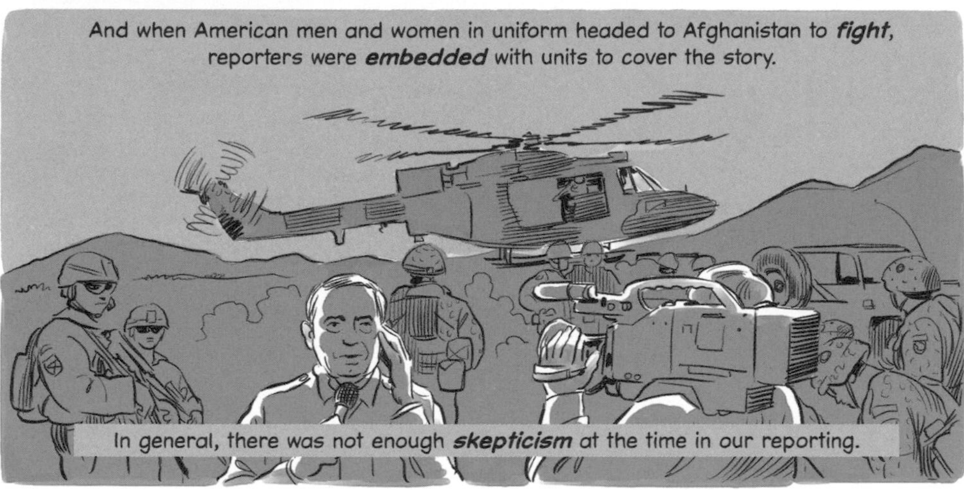
And when American men and women in uniform headed to Afghanistan to ***fight***, reporters were ***embedded*** with units to cover the story.
In general, there was not enough ***skepticism*** at the time in our reporting.

We should have asked ***harder questions*** about whether we were committing enough resources to the war, and whether the special operations-led campaign was the ***right approach***.

Then, almost immediately, we started hearing talk from ***high-level officials*** in the George W. Bush administration, especially ***Vice President Dick Cheney***, of a place that had been off the radar of most Americans for some time:
Iraq.

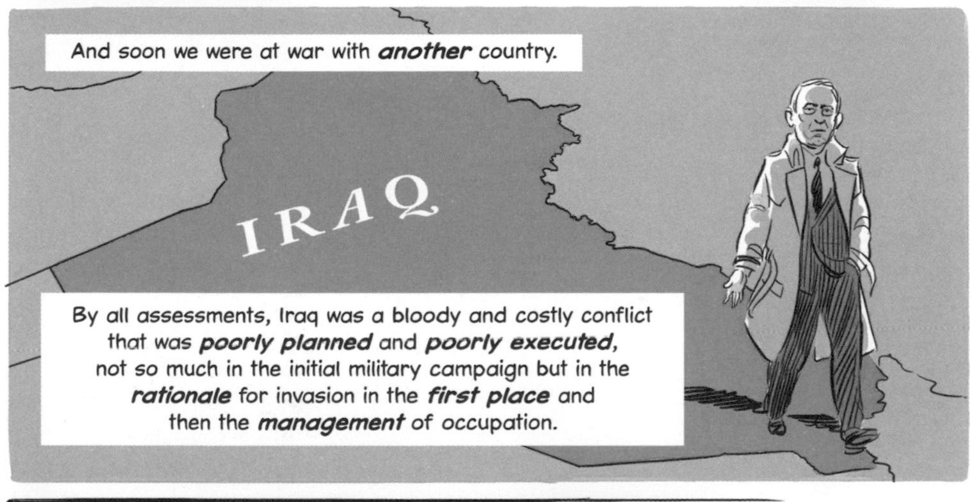
And soon we were at war with ***another*** country.
IRAQ
By all assessments, Iraq was a bloody and costly conflict that was ***poorly planned*** and ***poorly executed***, not so much in the initial military campaign but in the ***rationale*** for invasion in the ***first place*** and then the ***management*** of occupation.

Almost ***all*** of the press, ***myself*** included, accepted the selling of the war around "***weapons of mass destruction***" with far too little skepticism.

UNITED STATES
This wasn't simply a case of "fake news." It was a subtle propaganda, with just enough of an air of plausability to lull a nation into a war of choice.

And yet, despite the thin evidence, the press continued to use the term "WMD" up to and after the war.

Meanwhile, the links of Iraq to Al-Qaeda, which we now know were nonexistent, involved so much nuanced explanation of people and groups with foreign names that it was easy for the administration to sow confusion and sell its policies.

IRAQ WAR

And the press didn't do enough to investigate these claims.

As the military effort in Iraq became an increasingly fractious occupation, the press began to ask harder questions, despite the predictable blowback from the administration.

Much of what we now know about what happened in Iraq is because of great journalism.

But the policy decisions had already been made and the damage had already been done.

The war destabilized a region that was *already unstable.*
It is a *troubling lesson* about the dangers of unintended consequences.
In *wartime*, the American people tend to give an administration a lot of *latitude* in waging the fight, and for *good reason.*

Wars are *difficult affairs*, and it is easy to be an *armchair general.*
It is not the role of the press to suggest *military strategy* or actively undercut the *commander in chief.*
Our job is merely to *ask questions*, and if the answers are unsatisfactory, it is our *responsibility* to follow up with *more questions.*

In times of *strong patriotic fervor*, asking a question can be spun as *unpatriotic.*

At that time, there was a *feeling* that we shouldn't be making *too many waves.*

The problems with the press leading up to and during the early years of the Iraq War were also fueled by the changing economics of the American media landscape.
The business models that had sustained journalism—primarily print journalism, but also electronic media—began to crack under the stress of new technology.
TIME
At the time of the Iraq War, news outlets that had already been contending with shrinking revenues, job layoffs, and general uncertainty—
—now faced the challenges posed by the Internet.
The rate at which this digital revolution has upended the model of journalism cannot be overstated.
And as journalistic operations were consolidated into large corporations, reporters increasingly felt the pressure not to pursue unpopular story lines that might incur the wrath of the administration and thus—
—harm the bottom line and shareholder value.

We have seen how ***online advertising*** has proven elusive and disappointing—
—and efforts such as ***paywalls*** have not proven generally effective—
—as consumers can readily find news online for ***free***.

Newspapers ***in particular*** have suffered.
Many of the ***reasons*** that people had for maintaining their subscriptions to a paper can now all be found ***elsewhere***, instantaneously, and also, of course, for ***free***.

Meanwhile, cash cows like classified advertisements, which used to generate ***billions of dollars*** in annual revenue for newspapers—
—have largely ***dried up*** thanks to sites like ***Craigslist***.

The rise of ***social media*** as a primary news source has further ***put pressure*** on bottom lines.

But ***most important***, our evolving media landscape has made it more ***difficult*** for television news networks and newspapers to have the ***resources to employ*** editors and reporters.

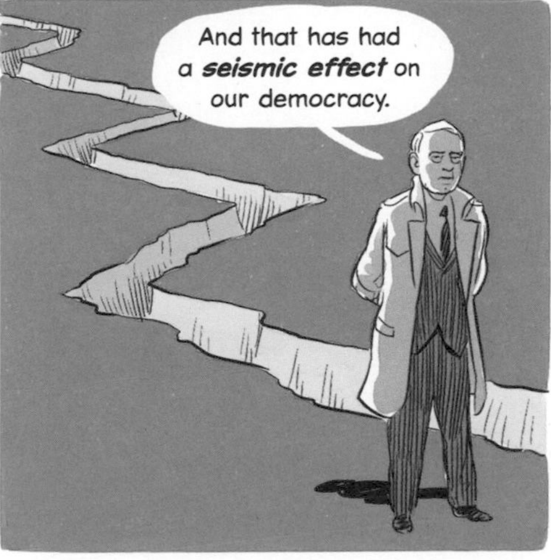
And that has had a ***seismic effect*** on our democracy.

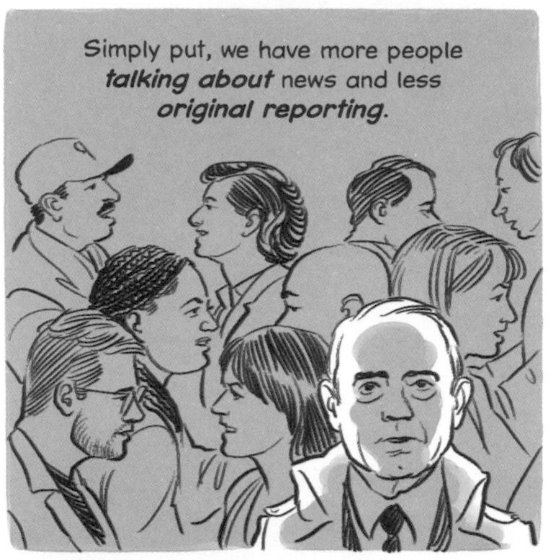
Simply put, we have more people talking about news and less original reporting.

Whether on television or online, there is no shortage of ***analysis***.

But ***analysis*** is only as good as the information that ***supports it***.

The ***deep cuts*** to newsrooms in print and electronic media have resulted in far ***fewer reporters*** waking up each morning deciding what story they will chase.

There is ***less investigative reporting*** and ***international coverage***.

What has gotten ***far less attention*** but has perhaps been the greatest loss to our democracy is the ***decimation*** that has come to ***local newspapers***.

These were always the ***engines*** that powered much of American journalism—

—as great ***local reporting*** would bubble up to the national newspapers and television.

Local newspapers also provided the check on local and state governments, reporting on mayors, city councils, school boards, and statehouses.

And with ***no coverage***, no one is keeping the people who ***work for us***—on those school boards or city councils—***accountable***.

MAYOR

I don't profess to know how to *fix* the business model—
The Atlantic
—but I am *encouraged* that long-form journalism is *flourishing* online.
Vox

There are many who believe that a *benefactor model* could be one solution, but it comes with its own *vulnerabilities.*
Washington Post
I hope we can find a *sustainable* means to better support online journalism.

In *recent years,* too many of those who covered politics in Washington—
—fell into a *Beltway mindset* of coziness with politicians of *both parties* and reporting that succumbed to *false equivalence,* as if every issue had two sides of equal worth.

But I have been *heartened* that the press is *emboldened* with a newfound resilience for *investigative journalism* and truth-telling.

Imagine where we would be today without the press working with dogged determination to hold those in power accountable.

We are seeing living proof of the wisdom of our Founders, who conceived of the First Amendment as a check on tyranny—an accountability that was missing in Orwell's vision in 1984.

But while these may be heroic times for journalists,
the outcome of the battle between propaganda and deception on the one hand and unbiased reporting on the other is far from clear.

No one has a monopoly on the truth.

The whole premise of our democracy is that truth and justice must win out.

And the role of a trained journalist is to get as close to the truth as is humanly possible.

Make no **mistake**.
We are being **tested**.
Without a vibrant, fearless **free press**, our great American experiment may **fail**.

3

community

When I was growing up, every ***woman*** who ***raised*** me, ***taught*** me, ***guided*** me, and ***loved*** me was born into a country that did not ***trust*** her with the ***right to vote***.
inclusion
African Americans were being ***lynched*** and subjected to state-sponsored ***segregation*** and ***disenfranchisement***.
The ***LGBTQ*** community were nearly always referred to by the ***vilest of slurs***, and the vast majority of them remained ***hidden***.
Disabled people were pitied, but there was no systematic effort to change public buildings, transportation, or sidewalks to make the world ***easier to navigate***.
America was a place where the privilege conferred on white, Protestant, straight, nondisabled men was not even ***questioned***. This privilege remains strong today, but it now must compete with a growing chorus calling for a ***fairer***, more ***inclusive*** nation.
Legally and socially, we have made ***great progress***, even if the ***summit*** of true equality and justice remains distant.

Tolerance is a prerequisite for a functional democracy.
But tolerance alone is not ***sufficient;***

it allows us to accept others without ***engaging*** with them—

—to feel smug and self-satisfied without ***challenging*** the boundaries within which many of us live.

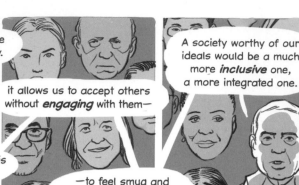

A society worthy of our ideals would be a much more ***inclusive*** one, a more integrated one.

This is a sentiment that itself stretches back to our founding. Our first ***national motto*** was
E PLURIBUS UNUM
"***From many, one.***" From many states, we are one nation.

Back in my childhood, the idea of an ***African American*** or a ***woman*** as president was a concept so completely implausible—
—that my peers and I never even ***bothered*** to talk about it.

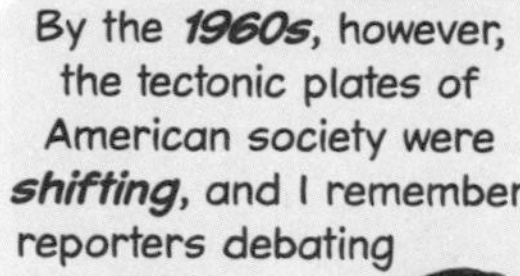

By the ***1960s***, however, the tectonic plates of American society were ***shifting***, and I remember reporters debating the issue.

But in the 1960s and 1970s, that started to change, as well. And with it, the idea of an African American or female president began to seem even more tangible.
These conversations were almost always conducted by ***white males*** only, as we made up the vast ***majority*** of the working press at the time.

Familiarity is a necessary ingredient for ***acceptance***.

But there was one ***marginalized group*** for whom there was almost no sense of a ***path*** to ***progress***.

If you had told us back in the 1960s and 1970s that there would be ***legal gay marriage*** in all fifty states, we would have been ***stunned***.

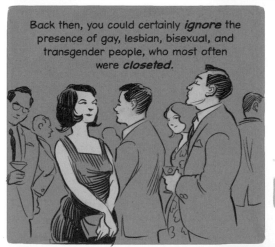

Back then, you could certainly ***ignore*** the presence of gay, lesbian, bisexual, and transgender people, who most often were ***closeted***.

It may be difficult for some younger readers to imagine, but for most of my life, the ***LGBTQ community*** was never discussed in "polite" company.

Horrible ***epithets*** for gay people were bandied about without a second thought.

The very theoretical idea of someone ***"like that"*** living in your neighborhood—
—let alone ***teaching your children***, was seen as a ***perverted*** threat to society.

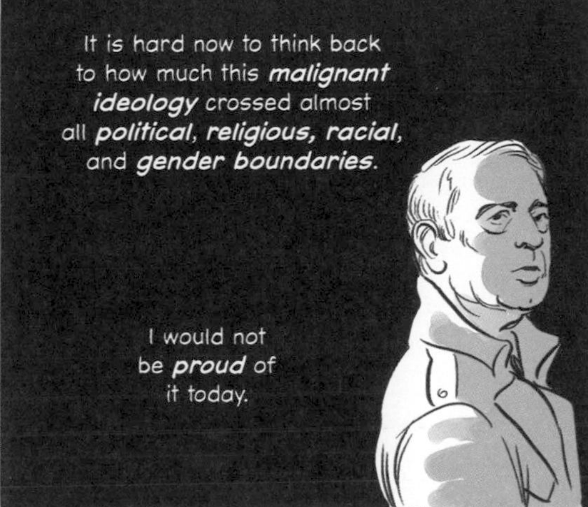
It is hard now to think back to how much this ***malignant ideology*** crossed almost all ***political***, ***religious***, ***racial***, and ***gender boundaries***.
I would not be ***proud*** of it today.

The report was filled with the **tropes of the times:** psychiatrists claiming homosexuality was a **mental condition**, provocative images of hustlers, and interviews with gay Americans in **anonymity**.
In 1967, two years before the **Stonewall riots** in New York City would bring gay rights to national prominence, CBS News aired a documentary hosted by **Mike Wallace** called *The Homosexuals*.

Most Americans are **repelled** by the mere notion of homosexuality.

The average homosexual, if there be such, is **promiscuous.** He is not interested in, nor capable of, a **lasting relationship** like that of a heterosexual marriage.

His **sex life**, his love life, consists of a series of chance encounters at the clubs and bars he **inhabits**.

I raise this not to take particular exception with Mr. Wallace. It was **brave** to even tackle the subject then, and the program also included ***sympathetic*** interviews with gay men talking publicly to a ***national audience*** for the ***first time***.

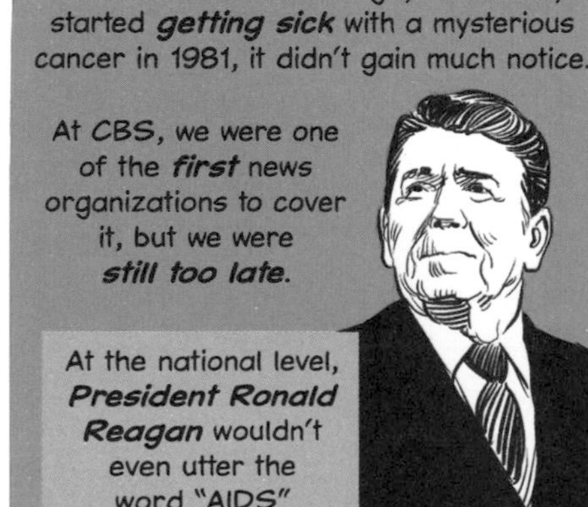
When members of the gay community started ***getting sick*** with a mysterious cancer in 1981, it didn't gain much notice.
At CBS, we were one of the ***first*** news organizations to cover it, but we were ***still too late***.
At the national level, ***President Ronald Reagan*** wouldn't even utter the word "AIDS" for ***years***.

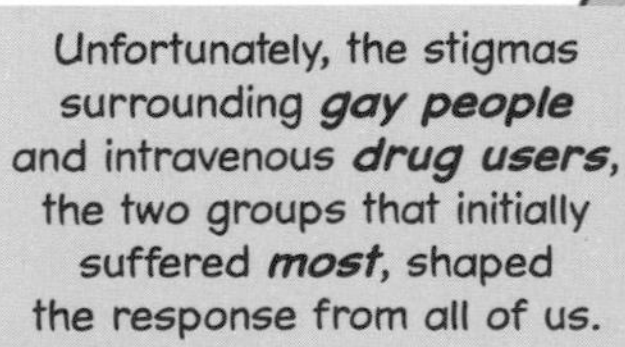
Our job as reporters, and the job of political leaders, is to confront ***hard truths*** without ***bias*** or prejudice.
Unfortunately, the stigmas surrounding ***gay people*** and intravenous ***drug users***, the two groups that initially suffered ***most***, shaped the response from all of us.

We knew how big a story AIDS was, but there was an ***effort*** among ***journalists*** from all walks to "broaden" the reporting.

When ***Ryan White***, a young ***hemophiliac*** from ***Kokomo, Indiana***, was diagnosed with AIDS after a ***blood transfusion***, the disease took on a more ***sympathetic*** face for the press.

It ***hurts my heart*** to write these words and think of all the ***thousands*** of gay men who suffered and died before and since.
Many lived under a cloud of ***shame***, shunned by former friends and family.

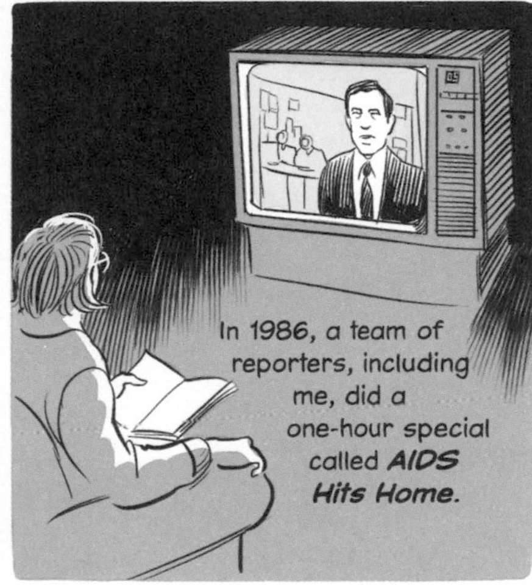
In 1986, a team of reporters, including me, did a one-hour special called ***AIDS Hits Home***.

It was certainly ***far from perfect***, but it was an improvement over *The Homosexuals* from twenty years earlier.

But as I look back now, the ***subtext*** was that America should care more broadly about AIDS because it was no longer just a ***gay disease***.

Those were the times in which we were ***living***, and we were ***not sensitive***.

LGBT
DEMAND EQUAL RIGHTS
ACT-UP
The societal change regarding LGBTQ rights **continues** to our present time.
As late as the Democratic primaries in the 2008 election, neither **Barack Obama** nor **Hillary Clinton** would publicly support same-sex marriage.
They still had to **"evolve"** on the issue or it was considered too **politically toxic.**
Both are now **solidly** pro-gay marriage, as is almost the entirety of the Democratic Party, and **even** many Republicans.

The **key**, I think—and it is not a **novel** or **original idea**—is that our progress with **LGBTQ rights** is due to greater inclusion with the rest of society.
We know that **homosexuality** is not limited to any race, religion, or socioeconomic class—
—it is part of **human diversity.**

Once people had the **courage** and support to come out of the closet, families across the country, rich and poor, black and white, rural and urban, were forced to confront what had **long remained hidden:**

sisters, brothers, sons, daughters—
—best friends, coworkers—
—even fathers and mothers—
—turned out to be **gay, lesbian, bisexual, queer**, and **transgender**.

Not all were accepting, and the tally of LGBT people rejected and disowned is large, and continues to grow. But many made room in their **moral universe** not only to tolerate LGBTQ people, but also to **include** them.

Like so many others in our country, I journeyed from ***ignorance*** to tolerance to ***inclusion.***
By the late 1990s, I had come to realize the ***undue challenges*** facing gay and lesbian people in American society, but the ***true burden*** many of them faced hadn't fully ***struck me.***

And then one day I was sitting in my office at CBS News when a close longtime colleague came in and shut the door—
I need to talk to you.

I'm gay.
In that moment I understood the ***courage*** it must have taken him to tell me this.

As we spoke, I could see his ***whole demeanor*** shift, as if a tightly wound spring was finally allowed to ***relax.***

Thankfully, we have, as a nation and as individuals, made ***meaningful steps*** in the right direction.
We must be ***vigilant*** and keep up the momentum, and there are ***new threats*** in the moment and on the ***horizon.***

Inclusion on ***race*** has been a very ***different journey***, and I worry that for all the progress we have made—
—we are ***stuck*** in the purgatory of ***tolerance***.

We have of late seen ***evidence*** of a great racial ***divide*** that remains, and in some ways even appears to be expanding—
—more than half a century after the major legislative ***victories*** in the ***civil rights movement***.

We are still ***largely segregated*** as a society, and our political divisions increasingly fall along lines of race.

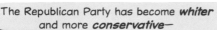

The Republican Party has become ***whiter*** and more ***conservative***—
—and the Democrats have become more ***diverse*** and ***progressive***.

Yes, we saw a historic moment in the ***2008 election*** with our first African American president, but how ***distant*** all the talk of a "post-racial America" seems today.
The long shadow of slavery, segregation, and ***racism*** still looms over this nation.

Several years ago I worked on a documentary on the public school system of ***Detroit***.

The city has become a ***potent symbol*** of so many of the challenges that face this country, race being ***first*** and ***foremost***.

But for the ***children*** growing up in the poverty of much of Detroit today, symbolism doesn't matter.

The documentary found a broken city of families struggling against the odds, of deserted neighborhoods, inadequate public transportation, and low-paying jobs.

Meanwhile the school system has been plagued by corruption and mismanagement.

Amid all this, one truth cannot be ignored: the Detroit public schools are almost entirely African American, and the schools in the surrounding suburbs are overwhelmingly white.
This is not an accident.

In 1974, the Supreme Court heard a case that centered on Detroit's schools, both in the city and in the surrounding communities.

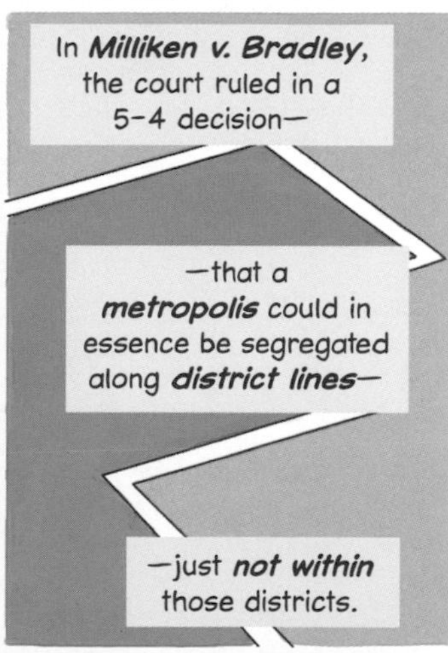
In Milliken v. Bradley, the court ruled in a 5-4 decision—
—that a metropolis could in essence be segregated along district lines—
—just not within those districts.

In other words, it was okay if there were real racial divisions, lines of exclusion, between suburbs and cities.

And that is the system we largely have today.

In a blistering dissent on the *Milliken* decision, ***Justice Thurgood Marshall*** predicted:
School district lines, however ***innocently*** drawn, will ***surely*** be perceived as ***fences*** to separate the races.

We have become a ***less inclusive*** nation as a result.

In our reporting for the documentary, I interviewed a remarkable young woman named ***Deanna Williams,*** who was a high school student at the time.

It's ***frustrating*** to know that I could be learning all of these things and I could be doing all of these things, and I ***can't.***

And people think... that the children in the Detroit Public Schools are stupid and brutish because of what they see on ***television.***

And it's ***not*** true.

We ***want*** to learn.

We want to be able to do what the ***other*** children are doing.

We want to have the ***same*** opportunities.

But they keep taking it ***away*** from us.

They keep—it's like they're keeping us ***down!***

And every day I want to know ***why.***
Why is this happening?

We titled the film *A National Disgrace*—
—not only because of the deep ***dysfunction*** of the Detroit schools—
—but because we as a nation ***allowed*** this to happen.

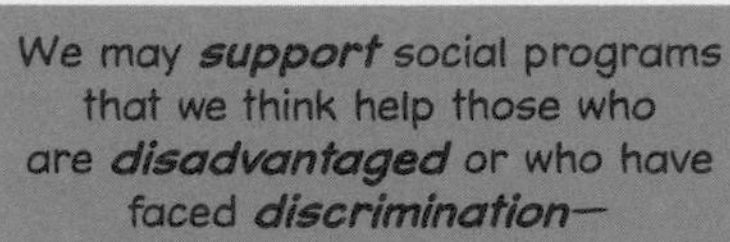
We may ***support*** social programs that we think help those who are ***disadvantaged*** or who have faced ***discrimination***—

—but if we do not ***fully engage*** in a spirit of inclusion on a ***personal*** level, we are failing.

If we are not actively trying to ***tear down*** the "fences to separate the races"—
—then we are ***all*** part of the ***problem.***

Building a more inclusive nation for ***women*** presents a ***unique*** set of ***hurdles*** (keeping in mind that LGBTQ women and women from racial minorities face ***multiple forms*** of discrimination).

The struggles women face in achieving equality remain both ***legal*** and ***cultural***.
In 2007, my reporting team and I investigated a story of ***female*** and ***minority custodians*** in the New York City public schools who claimed they had faced discrimination in the early 1990s.

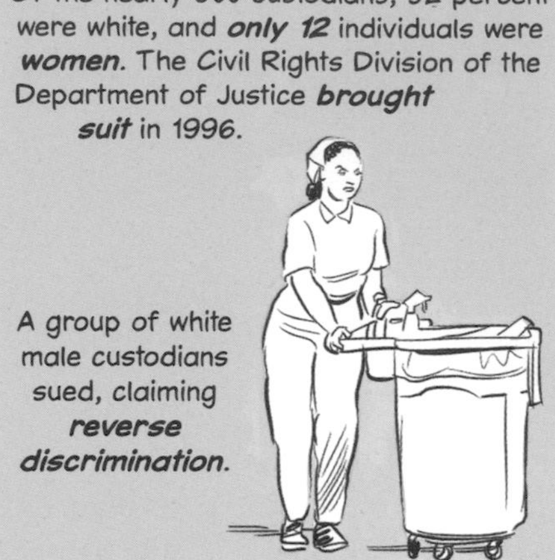
Of the nearly 900 custodians, 92 percent were white, and ***only 12*** individuals were ***women***. The Civil Rights Division of the Department of Justice ***brought suit*** in 1996.
A group of white male custodians sued, claiming ***reverse discrimination***.

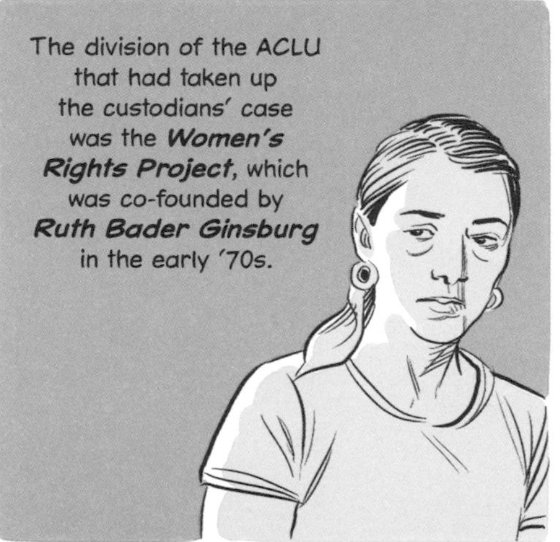
The division of the ACLU that had taken up the custodians' case was the ***Women's Rights Project***, which was co-founded by ***Ruth Bader Ginsburg*** in the early '70s.

Ginsburg directed the unit until she joined the ***federal bench*** in 1980—
—and during her time at the ACLU, in a series of ***landmark cases*** before the Supreme Court, she ushered in a ***new era*** of law for ***gender discrimination***.

When Ginsburg was nominated to the ***Supreme Court*** in 1993, 106 justices had preceded her, and only ***one***, the trailblazer ***Sandra Day O'Connor***, had been a woman.

Ginsburg is thoughtful, wise, and clearly blessed with a ***brilliant mind*** that has been honed and shaped through years of ***scholarship***.
There is ***no doubt*** that having ***women*** on the bench has had a ***profound effect***.

The more we are around people with a ***variety*** of life experiences—
—the more we can ***understand*** and ***value*** the needs and worth of our ***fellow citizens.***

In many ways, we have made ***important legal progress*** when it comes to ***women.***
As the proud father of a ***daughter*** who came of age in the wake of a growing feminist movement, I saw how she benefited, as did ***many*** students and athletes—
—from the famous Title IX of the ***Education Amendments Act*** of 1972.

That act stated: *"No person in the United States shall, on the basis of **sex**, be excluded from participation in, be denied the benefits of, or be subjected to discrimination under any education program or activity receiving Federal financial assistance."*
But it's ***one thing*** to have greater equality of opportunity under the law (itself an elusive goal), and ***another*** to see it happen in ***practice.***
As women have pushed more and more for access and equity, we can no longer ignore them. And that, in itself, is a form of progress.

When I was young, we heard often of how the United States was a great ***melting pot.***
It is a ***fine metaphor*** as far as it goes.

But ***inclusion,*** not assimilation, should be the ***key concept*** in seeking, ever seeking—
—a more ***perfect*** national union.

Our own history has shown that we are **stronger** as a **mosaic** than a melting pot.

empathy

I am not sure if the word ***"empathy"*** was in either of my parents' vocabularies.

It wasn't the kind of word one ***heard*** growing up in my neighborhood in ***Houston***.

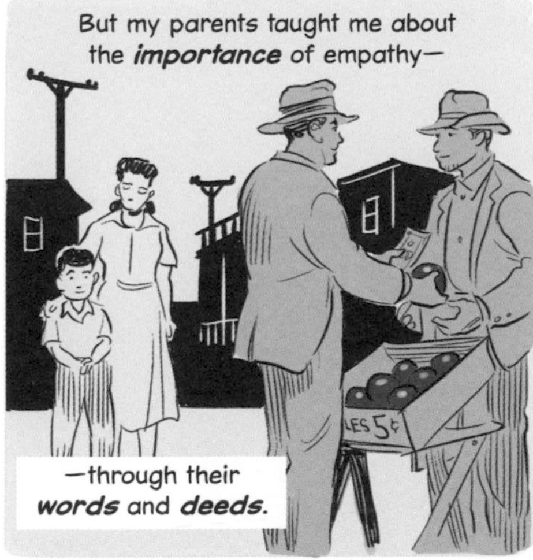

But my parents taught me about the importance of empathy—
LES 5¢
—through their words and deeds.

And they made it clear that it was part of the glue that held together our family, our neighborhood, our community—
—and the United States itself.

My ***earliest memories*** are of times of despair and the ***Great Depression***.

We lived in the ***Heights neighborhood***.

It was considered a ***rough***, tough neighborhood, and there was only one street—a ***dirt street***—between our house and the ***open country***.

Our house was nothing to ***brag*** about—

—but at least it had four sturdy walls, with two bedrooms, a small living room, a small kitchen, and one bath.
Across our street was a poor frame house in a state of semicollapse.

A half block down lived a family who didn't even have a proper house. Their floor was dirt.

Nobody in either of these families had a ***job.***

That was not ***unusual*** in our neighborhood during the Depression.

And the families that were ***lucky*** enough to have work usually had only meager ***part-time*** jobs.

CAFE

PART-TIME HELP WANTED DISHWASHER

A full-time job like the one my father had working the ***oil fields*** was ***rare*** and considered a ***blessing,*** no matter the pay, the hours, or the amount of backbreaking labor it entailed.

This was what the ***United States of America*** was like not that long ago:
a ***country*** where families struggled to live on dirt streets, with dirt floors and little or ***no income*** to pay the ***grocery*** or ***medical bills.***
None of this was considered particularly ***unusual*** at the time.
It was just the way things ***were.***

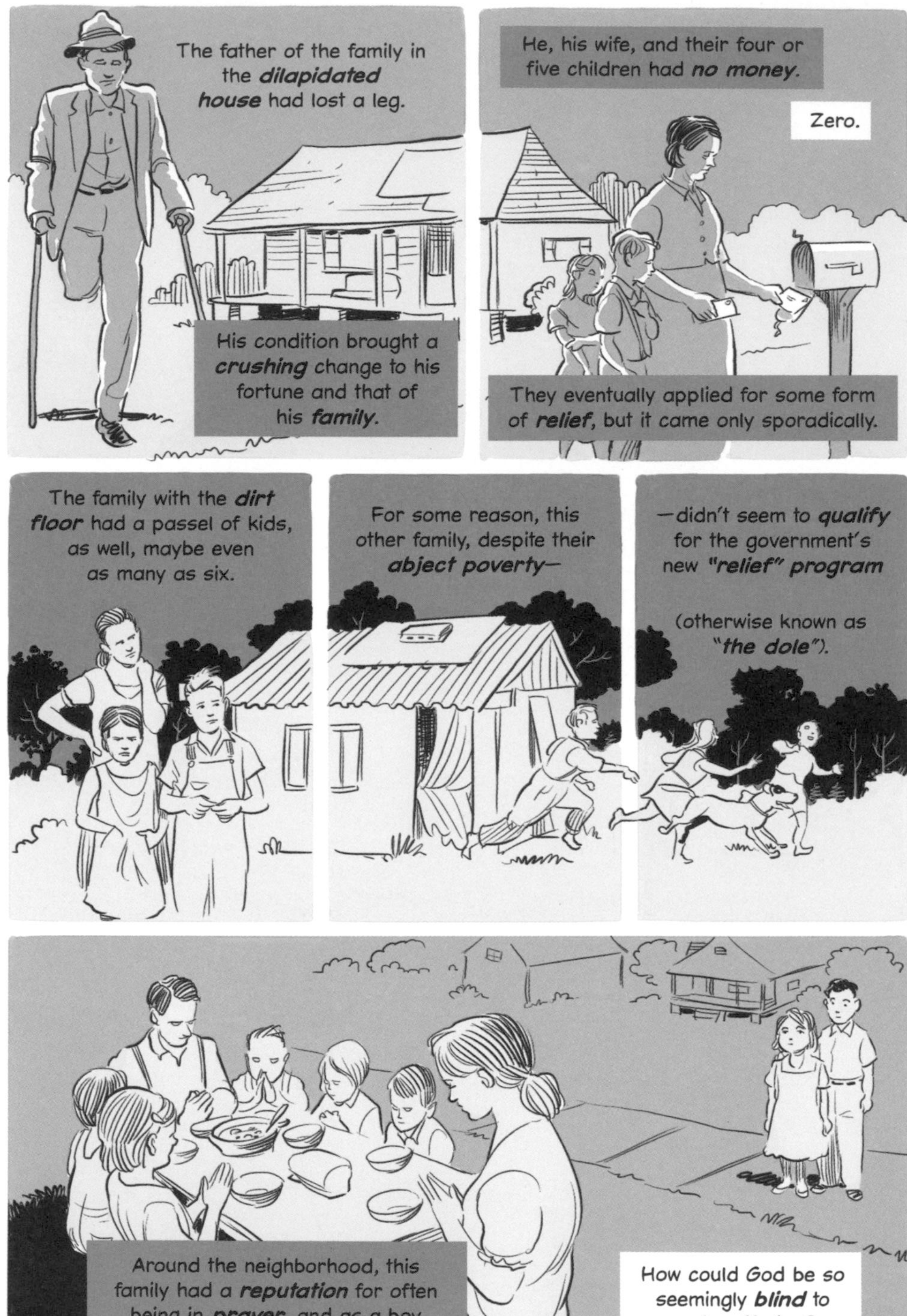
The father of the family in the *dilapidated house* had lost a leg.
His condition brought a *crushing* change to his fortune and that of his *family*.
He, his wife, and their four or five children had *no money*.
Zero.
They eventually applied for some form of *relief*, but it came only sporadically.
The family with the *dirt floor* had a passel of kids, as well, maybe even as many as six.
For some reason, this other family, despite their *abject poverty*—
—didn't seem to *qualify* for the government's new *"relief" program*
(otherwise known as "*the dole*").
Around the neighborhood, this family had a *reputation* for often being in *prayer*, and as a boy I wondered:
How could God be so seemingly *blind* to such suffering?

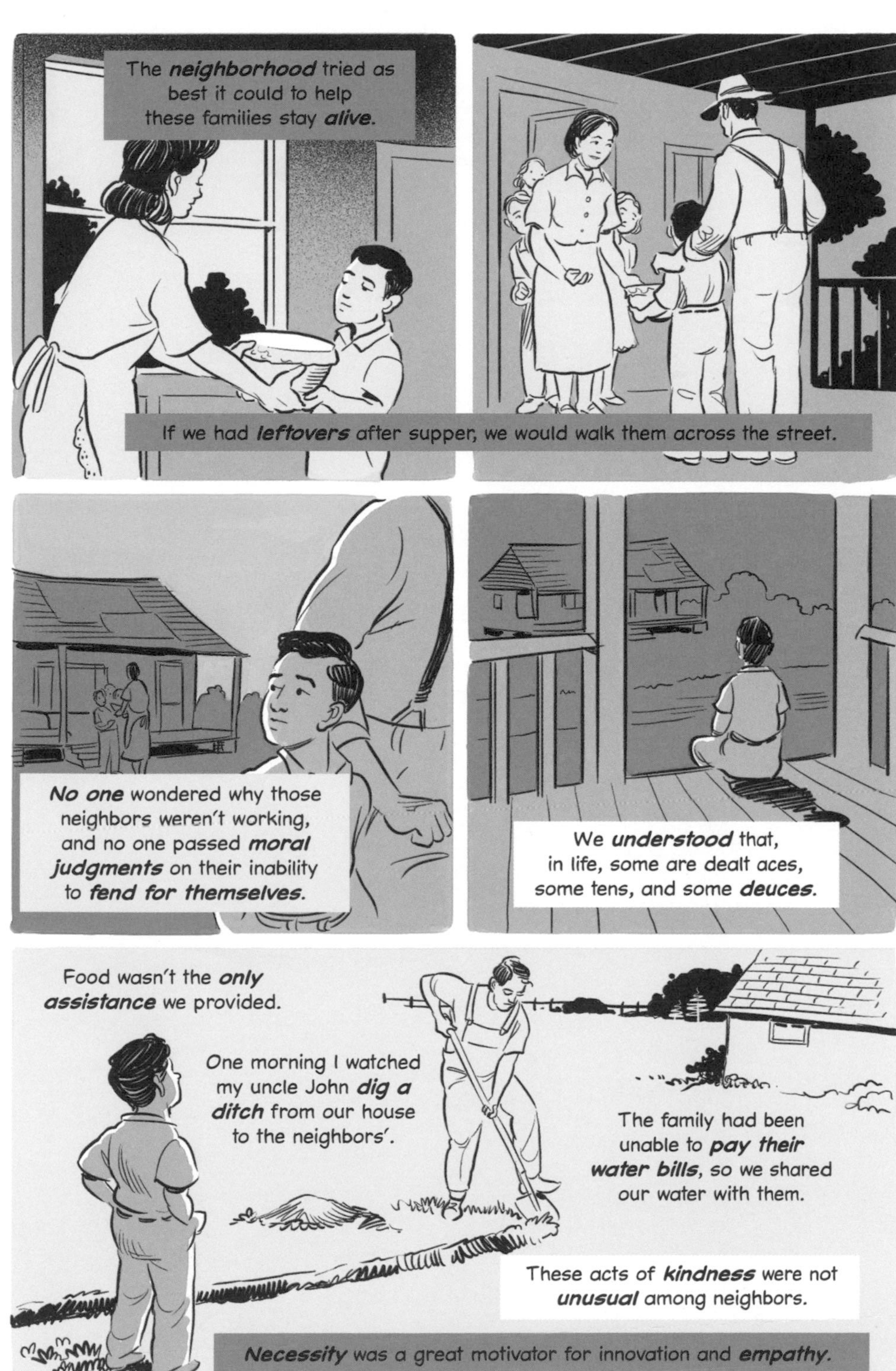
The neighborhood tried as best it could to help these families stay alive.
If we had leftovers after supper, we would walk them across the street.
No one wondered why those neighbors weren't working, and no one passed moral judgments on their inability to fend for themselves.
We understood that, in life, some are dealt aces, some tens, and some deuces.
Food wasn't the only assistance we provided.
One morning I watched my uncle John dig a ditch from our house to the neighbors'.
The family had been unable to pay their water bills, so we shared our water with them.
These acts of kindness were not unusual among neighbors.
Necessity was a great motivator for innovation and empathy.

What sticks with me more than even those acts of kindness was how my mother *talked* to me about it.
I was an inquisitive child (perhaps not surprising considering my later path in life), and I was always asking *questions*.

I asked why we gave those families *gifts* at Christmas when we ourselves didn't have much.
It's because we feel sorry for them, *right?*

We do not feel *sorry* for them.

We understand how they *feel*.

It was a lesson that is so *seared in my mind*, I can see her face and I can hear her tone of voice as if it were *yesterday*.

What my family did was not *heroic*.
I like to think of it more as *neighborly*.

And it was in line with a national ethos in those *dark days*, repeated countless times in countless communities across the country.

We understood that those who were *suffering* weren't *lazy* or lacking the *desire* to do better.
Fate had the potential to slap *any* of us.

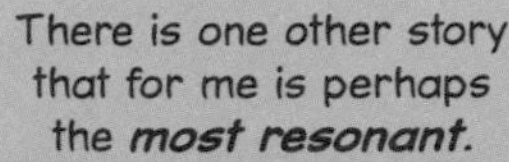
There is one other story that for me is perhaps the ***most resonant***.

It is of a boy, a few years older than I, who lived near us and had a ***gifted artistic sensibility***.

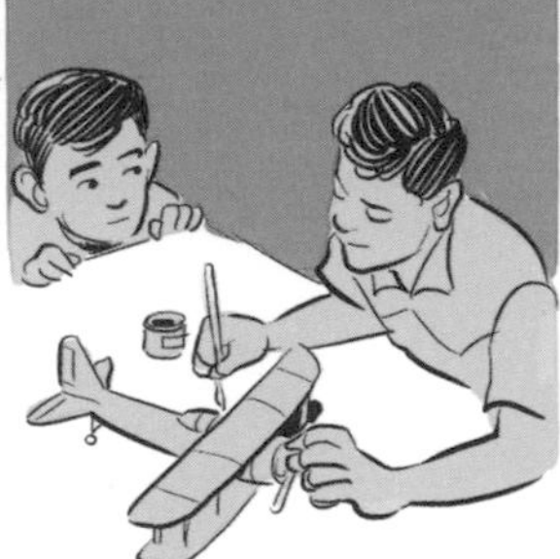
He was the kind of kid who could ***draw*** almost anything.
In different circumstances, he might have grown up to show his work in ***galleries***.

He had also been a strong student and a wonderful ***athlete***, winning all the footraces in the neighborhood and dominating sandlot baseball.

But his family was in ***dire economic straits***, so he quit school at fifteen to start looking for a job to ***support them***.
HELP
WANTED
APPLY
WITHIN

He never found much work other than a few projects ***helping out*** as a bricklayer.
What he did start to find was ***trouble***. He began smoking and running with the wrong crowd.

Before long, he became ill with what I believe was some respiratory ailment and went into the ***hospital***.
When I visited him, I saw the ***shell*** of a young man, in many ways still a boy.

I had looked up to him as one ***blessed*** with talent and grace, and here he was, completely ***defeated*** by a life that had once held such ***promise***.
Shortly thereafter he ***died***.

I attributed it to a ***broken heart***, and I imagine him taking his final breaths with ***flashes*** of what could have been, what ***might*** have been.

It is perhaps not surprising that *Nazi Germany* and *Imperial Japan* looked at a nation so traumatized and felt they could *defeat* us.
Of course, history turned out *differently*.

The *same* generation that had been driven to such *depths* in the 1930s *rose up* to push back the forces of *totalitarianism* in a two-ocean *global war* in the 1940s.

Perhaps those authoritarians, who felt *no empathy* for their own people or those they *conquered*, underestimated the strength of our empathy.

Empathy builds *community*.
Communities *strengthen* a country and its resolve and will to fight back.

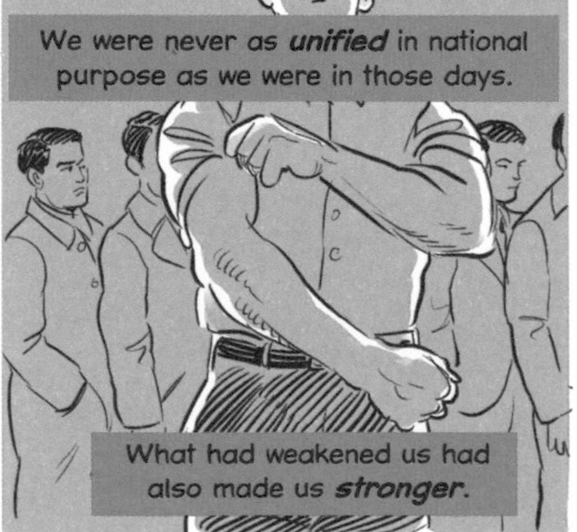
We were never as *unified* in national purpose as we were in those days.
What had weakened us had also made us *stronger*.

I remember a major push to organize for *civil defense*, as there was a great fear of a German or Japanese *invasion*.
VOLUNTE
HERE
Almost everyone, truly everyone, regardless of age, race, or economic status, *rushed* to *come together* and help as soon as word came out.

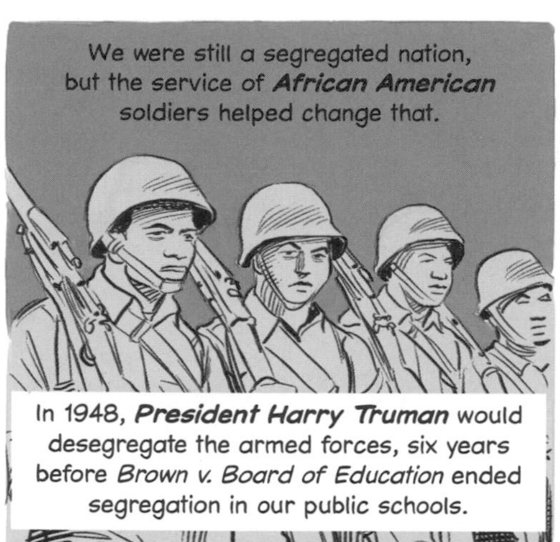
We were still a segregated nation, but the service of African American soldiers helped change that.
In 1948, President Harry Truman would desegregate the armed forces, six years before Brown v. Board of Education ended segregation in our public schools.

Indeed, this sweep of empathy continued after the war.
One of the best foreign policy efforts in American history was to help rebuild Europe and Japan.

Our enemies became our friends through an acknowledgment of the common bonds of humanity.
The postwar world order was built on that foundation.

And when the GIs returned home, we treated them empathetically, as well.

The Servicemen's Readjustment Act of 1944, more commonly known as the GI Bill, was one of the greatest pieces of social legislation in our nation's history.
Among other benefits, the GI Bill ensured that servicemen's tuitions to college or technical school were fully paid.
Empathy makes for wise foreign and domestic policy.

When I consider the forces that have led to our **greatest moments** of **progress**, I do not think it is a surprise that a great spasm of **empathetic legislation** came in the midst of the **Great Depression.**
The beginning of **Social Security** is the most notable example—
SOCIAL SECURITY
—but there were a **host** of other **programs** that aimed to bring relief and the dignity of work to a populace in **desperate need.**
WPA
Many of these endeavors fell under the so-called **alphabet agencies,** federal programs created by President Franklin Roosevelt to combat the Great Depression.
TVA
SEC
This effort was widely popular and seen as the worthy and **necessary** actions of a government in touch with the **needs** of the people it served.
FLSA

The ***second wave*** of such legislation came in the 1960s, and I don't think it is coincidental that this happened as the children of the ***Great Depression*** and ***World War II*** grew into adulthood.

Efforts to improve racial justice, labor rights, antipoverty programs, education, medical care, and many other needs began under President John F. Kennedy's "***New Frontier***"–

—and peaked with President Lyndon Johnson's "***Great Society***"

The scope of legislation from this time is still staggering:

the ***Civil Rights Act***, the ***Voting Rights Act***, ***Medicare***, and ***Medicaid***, among others.

Note that ***most*** of these laws were passed with considerable—sometimes ***overwhelming***—bipartisan support.

We knew of no other world than one of hardship, and so we did not realize growing up how dire and anomalous the situation was.
I cannot imagine there was a more conducive environment in which to learn the lessons of empathy.

Today these kinds of empathetic programs are associated with big government bureaucracies.

But the spirit of *empathy* with which they were created has been *lost*.

Empathy is a *deeply personal* emotion.
It is about the feeling one has for one's *fellow human beings*.

Transferring responsibilities to *government* is often necessary, but it creates a *distance* between us and those who need help.

And if this impulse of forgoing our *individual* responsibilities is left unchecked, it absolves us—
—from our own *responsibility* as citizens to form a more empathetic union with others.

I worry that our nation today suffers from a *deficit* of empathy, and this is *especially true* of many in positions of *national leadership*.

It is a phenomenon that is *born from*, and that exacerbates, the broader *divisions* tearing at our republic.

We see a rising **tribalism** along cultural, ethnic, economic class, and geographic lines.
We live in a self-selected **bubble** of friends, neighbors, and colleagues. It is too easy to **forget** how important it is to try to walk in the shoes of others.

Very few families **escaped** the **wounds** of the Great Depression and World War II.
In the intervening decades, however, the wealthy and the powerful largely have been **protected** from economic, social, and military upheavals—
—by a **shield** of immunity.

A commonality of understanding has been **lost**. Where once the **American experience** was one of a spectrum from the rich to the poor—
—now we live in **pockets** that insulate us from others.

We have more in the ranks of the **extremely wealthy**, many fewer in the middle economic class, and a larger pool falling further and further **behind**.
HELP
GOD BLESS

So we grow more **isolated** and less empathetic.
The **threads** stitching our union together begin to **fray**.

We **see** others, but we cannot imagine what their lives are actually **like**.
We don't even think we should have to **bother**.

Empathy is not only a personal feeling; it can be a ***potent force*** for political and social change.
And thus the suppression or denial of empathy is a ***deliberate*** part of a cynical political calculus.

Dividing people and stoking animosity can ***pave a path*** to power—
—and in many recent elections it ***has.***

SAVE THE PLANET
CLIMATE CHANGE
BUILD THE WALL
END ABORTION
STRIKE
TEACHERS
EQUAL RIGHTS
But these divisions inevitably come at the ***expense*** of the long-term ***health*** and ***welfare*** of the nation as a whole.

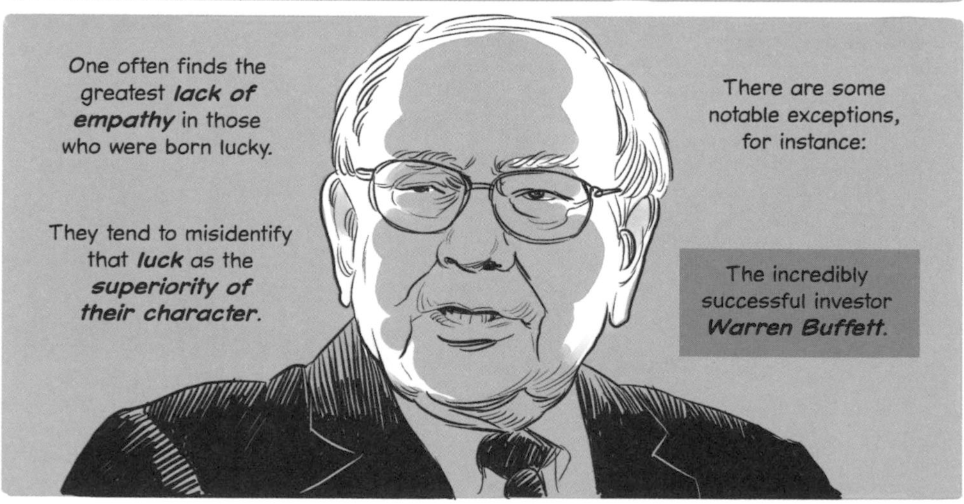
One often finds the greatest ***lack of empathy*** in those who were born lucky.
They tend to misidentify that ***luck*** as the ***superiority of their character.***
There are some notable exceptions, for instance:
The incredibly successful investor ***Warren Buffett.***

He once speculated to a group of students about what would *happen* if,

before birth, a genie gave us the opportunity to *choose* the political, economic, and social system into which we would be *born*.

One catch.

Just before you emerge from the womb, you have to go through a huge bucket with *seven billion slips, one for each human.*

Dip your hand in and *that is what you get*—you could be born *intelligent* or *not intelligent*, born *healthy* or *disabled*, born *black* or *white*, born in the *U.S.* or in *Bangladesh*, etc.

You have *no idea* which slip you will get. Not knowing which slip you are going to get, *how would you design the world?*

It is a wonderful thought experiment that lays out a provocative case for empathy.
Now take a moment to imagine the most sanctimonious of our current national voices.

How would these men and women fare in such a lottery as Buffett outlines?
What would their message be if they themselves had been born under far different circumstances?

These people are in dire need of ***humility***.
A humility bathed in the refreshing waters of ***empathy***.
We can ***all*** afford to ***drink more*** from that spring, as well.

immigration
No one can deny that the United States is now, and has always been, a nation of immigrants—
—even if the issue of immigration has become one of the most contentious and divisive of our current age.
In the Houston of my childhood, there was a significant population of African Americans, as well as Mexicans, with the southern border not far away.
There were undoubtedly small immigrant communities in Houston, but none of these groups made a sizeable impression on my young consciousness.
Little attention was paid in my school or upbringing to the means by which their ancestors had arrived in the Americas.

But later, when I was wooing my wife, *Jean*, I traveled out to meet her *family* in the deep hinterland of Texas.

Hers was a place of *open vistas*, where the scrub oaks far outnumbered the *human inhabitants*.

Jean came from a people known as the *Wends*, a Lutheran minority of Slavic ancestry who had been living in Germany and had faced *cultural and religious persecution*.

After settling in Texas, they sent back *glowing reports* of vast horizons, of both geography and *opportunity*.
This was *enough* for the entire congregation to make the dangerous passage across the great Atlantic in the *mid-nineteenth century*.

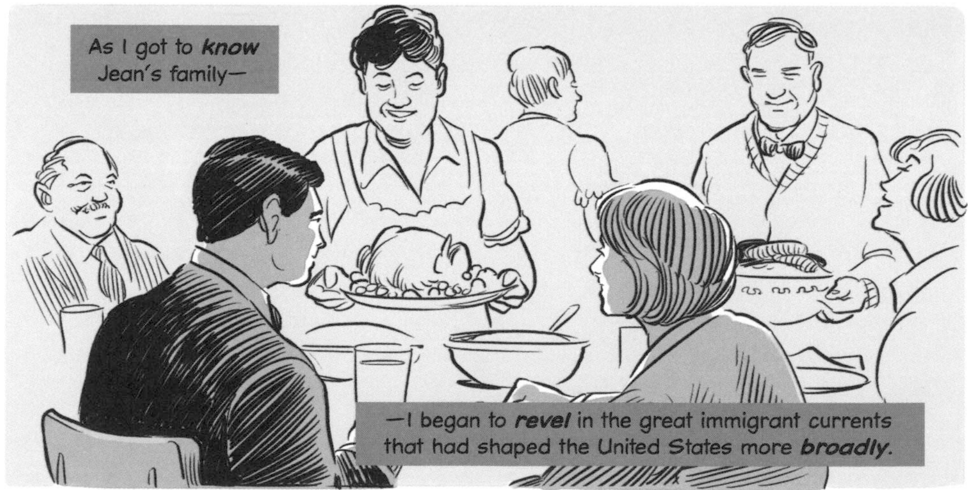
As I got to *know* Jean's family—
—I began to *revel* in the great immigrant currents that had shaped the United States more *broadly*.

From Jean's relatives, I learned that ***moving here*** did not require erasing a ***pride*** in one's ***ancestry***.
I saw how thoroughly these families ***embraced*** their American identity—
—they were ***patriots***, just like the people with whom I had grown up.
This is one of the greatest lessons of our nation's improbable makeup: A ***united citizenry*** can be ***quilted together*** from so many different ***cultural fabrics***.
I was already in my twenties, but I was ***realizing*** I had a lot to learn about a country I ***loved deeply***.

We have all come here from ***somewhere else***, and the vast majority of us are only a few generations removed from another land.

Even the ancestors of the ***Native Americans*** are believed to have come across a land bridge from Asia.

Of course, not ***all migrations*** have been ***voluntary***; many are here because their ancestors were ***ripped*** from their homelands in Africa and carried across the ocean in ***bondage***.

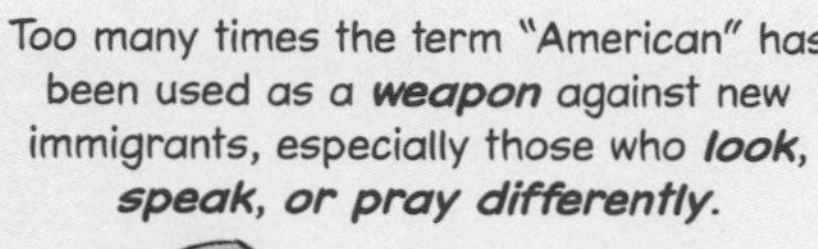
Too many times the term "American" has been used as a ***weapon*** against new immigrants, especially those who ***look, speak, or pray differently***.

And yet the ***noblest ideals*** of our country is that anybody from anywhere can be an ***American***.

This has been, and continues to be, an ***eternal battle*** between our demons and angels for the ***soul*** of the United States.

A nation that ***proclaimed*** "all men are created equal"—
—but that defined many men as ***three-fifths*** of a whole. And where women of all races were barred from voting.

The ***debate*** over immigration takes many forms, and some of them are ***worth*** considering.
There are also ***many*** hard questions.

How do we handle ***undocumented*** immigrants—
—not ***only*** the ones who have crossed our southern border—

—but ***also those*** who have overstayed visas?
VISA

How do we continue to welcome ***skilled workers*** who can benefit our ***economy***—
—without ***taking jobs away*** from American citizens capable of doing the work but who might demand a ***higher wage***?

How do we contend with the fact that many undocumented workers do ***difficult and dangerous*** jobs—
—in agriculture, construction, and service that most Americans ***do not seem*** to want to do themselves?

How do we balance ***empathy*** for refugees seeking asylum with ***security*** concerns?

Immigration will always be a complicated and ***perplexing*** issue, especially if we remain a country that is perceived as a ***promised land***.
That is the spirit that drew most of our ***ancestors***, and hopefully we will ***remain*** such a nation.

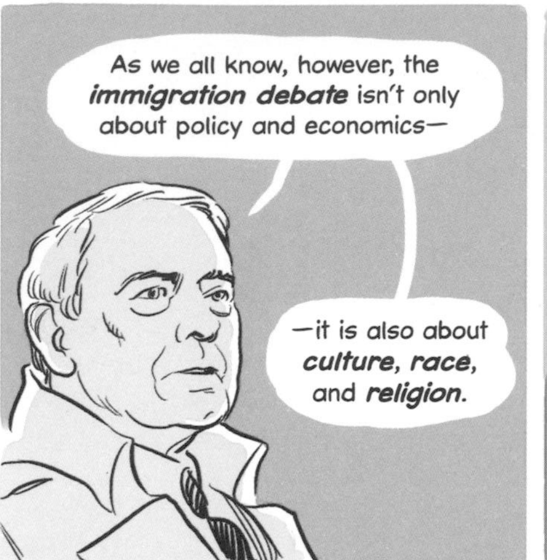
As we all know, however, the immigration debate isn't only about policy and economics—
—it is also about culture, race, and religion.

In the early days of the republic, the country needed settlers, so nearly anyone could immigrate.
Then, as the country started to grow and be seen as a land of opportunity, a big wave of immigration began in the decades before the Civil War.

Most were from Northern and Central Europe, and many were ***Catholics***—particularly from Germany and Ireland.

This sparked a ***fierce backlash*** of anti-immigrant and anti-Catholic sentiments.

It is ***ironic*** that some who question the "Americanness" of more ***recent*** arrivals are ***themselves*** descendants of those who were labeled "un-American" in the ***past***.

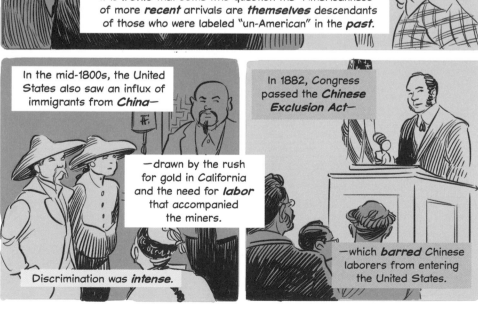

In the mid-1800s, the United States also saw an influx of immigrants from ***China***—

—drawn by the rush for gold in California and the need for ***labor*** that accompanied the miners.

Discrimination was ***intense***.

In 1882, Congress passed the ***Chinese Exclusion Act***—

—which ***barred*** Chinese laborers from entering the United States.

Congress passed sharp ***quotas*** on ***immigration*** in the 1920s ***favoring*** people from Northern Europe.

As Jewish refugees started to ***pour out*** of Europe to escape fascism, the United States ***tightened*** its borders and even turned some ships ***away,*** sending men, women, and children back to their ***deaths.***

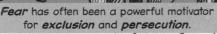

This ***xenophobia*** at the time of World War II led our government to round up and detain Japanese American citizens.
Fear has often been a powerful motivator for ***exclusion*** and ***persecution.***

These days, ***Muslims*** find themselves particularly under ***attack,*** not only by discriminatory new government ***immigration policies***—
—but also in schools, public spaces, and other avenues of daily life where their ***fellow citizens*** often make negative assumptions about their ***religion*** and reasons for being here.

Never mind that immigrants are ***rarely*** responsible for violent acts.
Instead we have seen time and again that immigrants and their children are ***eager*** to ***serve*** their new nation.

In recent years, when I reported from *distant* and *dangerous* military outposts in *Iraq* and *Afghanistan*, I saw a *great diversity* of surnames stitched into uniforms—and the pride of service in *diverse faces.*
CHAV
AZIZ
Patriotism and *sacrifice* know no ethnicity, race, or religion.
And it has *always* been thus.
There should be *no question* about whether our *newest* Americans are willing to *sacrifice* for their adopted country.

When I moved to New York in 1962, most of the immigration was still **European.**

Certain nationalities coalesced around **certain trades,** and I found that the **soundmen's union** was almost exclusively **Eastern European.**

Around the CBS newsroom, at drinks after work, and out on assignment, much of our banter was hardly politically correct, and there was a lot of **ethnic stereotyping** in our jokes.

But I remember being struck by how **collegial** it all felt.
In the news business, like the army, you can't get much done if you don't **work together.**

This was also the first time I really got to know Jewish Americans, starting when **Bernie Birnbaum** took me under his wing.
He was different from me in **every way** imaginable—

—native New Yorker, the son of **Russian** immigrants, Fulbright Scholar.
We **instantly** became dear friends.

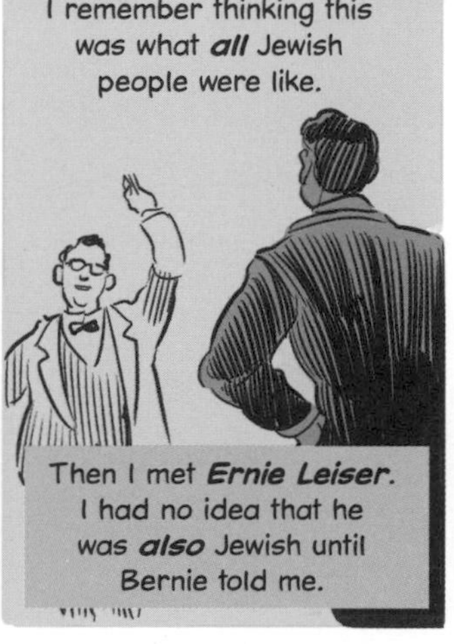
I remember thinking this was what **all** Jewish people were like.
Then I met **Ernie Leiser.** I had no idea that he was **also** Jewish until Bernie told me.

I was learning that **real people** didn't fall neatly into **stereotypes,** a lesson that many need to **revisit** these days.

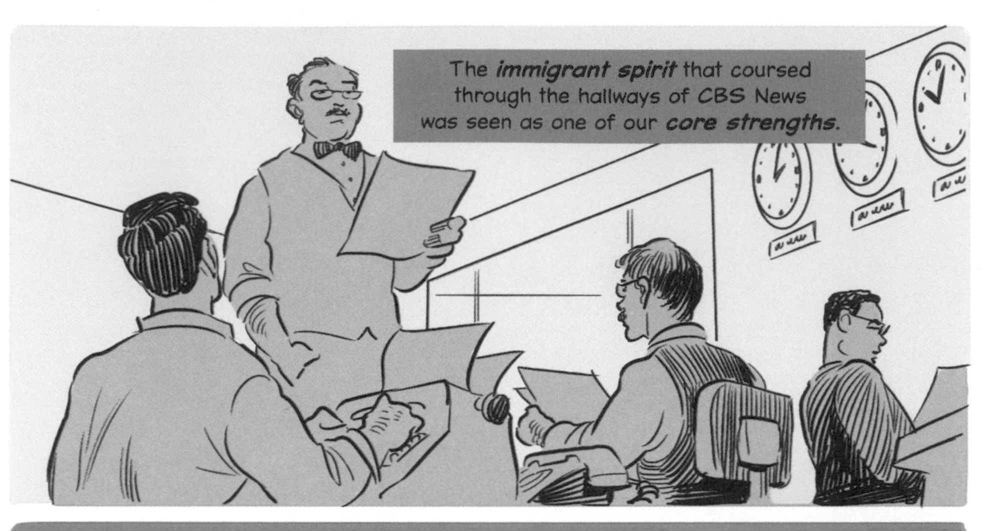
The *immigrant spirit* that coursed through the hallways of CBS News was seen as one of our *core strengths.*

What we didn't know at the time was that a ***sea change*** was coming that would ***transform*** the United States forever.

On October 3, 1965, President Lyndon Johnson traveled to ***Liberty Island*** in the harbor of New York and signed a ***sweeping change*** to America's immigration laws.

At the feet of the monumental statue that had welcomed so many of the ***huddled masses*** to our shores—

—Johnson ***undid*** a system that had been in place since the ***anti-immigrant backlash*** of the 1920s.

The **new law** eliminated immigration **quotas** based on race, ethnicity, and nation of origin.
Instead, it set up **different** preferential criteria, such as having a **relative** who was a U.S. citizen or legal resident and work in a profession with **specialized skills**.

This **system** violated the basic principle of American democracy—the principle that **values and rewards** each man on the basis of his merit as a man...
Our beautiful America was built by a nation of **strangers**. From a hundred different places or more they have **poured forth** into an empty land, joining and blending in one mighty and irresistible **tide**.

As a result, individuals from Asia, Africa, the Caribbean, South America, and many other far-flung locations have immigrated to the United States, and their **extended families** have followed.
The resulting change in American **demographics** has been revolutionary.

Over the course of our nation's history, waves of immigration have time and again expanded the definition of what it means to be an American.
And each time, eras of permissive immigration—
—were bracketed by eras of deep restrictions.
Opponents have all used the same version of the same argument:
America will no longer be America.
They have always been wrong.

But we cannot deny that *change* can create feelings of *anxiety* and unease among those who see America, as they know it, slipping away.

There are *legitimate* concerns, but if politicians of all persuasions tried to speak to audiences beyond their own voting base and argued that we must root for *prosperity* among all Americans—
—I suspect *much* of this anxiety could be *diminished*.

In 1986, *President Ronald Reagan* oversaw the passage of a bill that allowed *millions* of people living in this country without documentation—
—to come out of the *shadows*.

He said in a *debate* against Walter Mondale:
I believe in the idea of amnesty for those who have *put down roots* and who have lived here even though sometime back they may have entered *illegally*.
With the right *leadership,* I believe we could find *similar* compromise today.

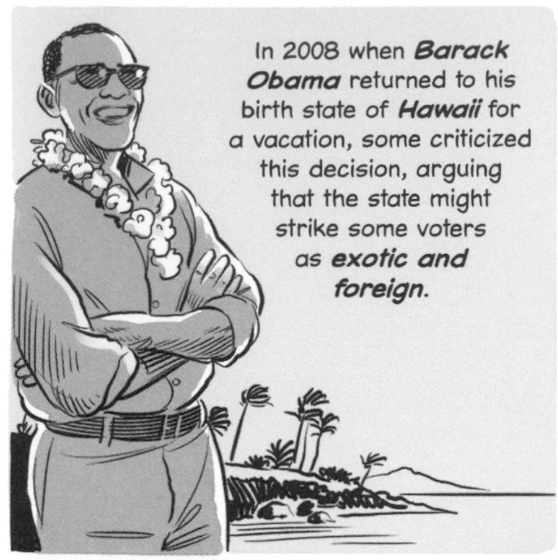
In 2008 when Barack Obama returned to his birth state of Hawaii for a vacation, some criticized this decision, arguing that the state might strike some voters as exotic and foreign.

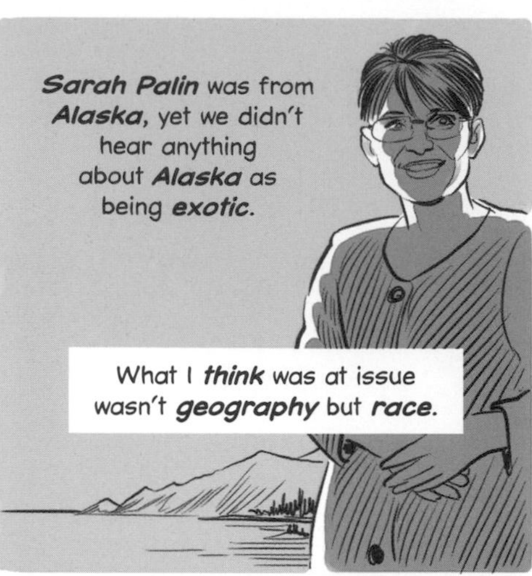
Sarah Palin was from Alaska, yet we didn't hear anything about Alaska as being exotic.
What I think was at issue wasn't geography but race.

Hawaii is the most diverse state in the union, the result of waves of Asian immigration.
By contrast, Alaska is predominantly white, save for a considerable population of Native Americans.

Today we see an eagerness among some of our elected officials—
—buoyed by passionate segments of the voting public—to erect new barriers to immigration.
But these efforts will not stop the demographic momentum already underway in the United States.
If anything, I believe that demonizing the most recent arrivals to our shores will only, over time, galvanize the political will of the majority of Americans who understand the true legacy of our history.

When I walk around this great land, in small towns and big cities, bus stations and airports, baseball stadiums and art museums—
—I see an America that has expanded beyond the wildest dreams of its founders.
We are a people of energy and purpose, a blended land of ever-increasing diversity that has so far proven the strength and wisdom of our great experiment.

4

exploration

science
"Everyone is entitled to his own opinion, but not to his own facts."
—Senator Daniel Patrick Moynihan
I *shudder* to think what the late senator would make of America *today*.
God forbid, but if this nation ultimately *fails*,
I believe it will be because *opinions, propaganda, and superstitions* replaced *facts* as the basis for our *governance*.
By doing so, we will have undercut a *key strength* of the United States over the course of its history—
—one that receives too little attention: *science*.

When I say "***science,***" I mean more than simply the study of biology or physics, or how much we fund ***basic research***.

Fundamentally, science is about a method of ***understanding*** our world through ***observation***, ***experimentation***, and ***analysis***.

It's about allowing ***facts*** to win out over ***prejudice***, no matter how ***deeply entrenched***.
Charles Darwin
ORIGIN OF SPECIES

We are seeing these values ***under attack***—
SAVE OUR PLANET
CLIMATE CHANGE IS
—from ***climate-change denial*** to the questioning of our own government's statistics when they prove to be ***politically inconvenient***.

This state of affairs is putting the future of our nation at ***risk***.
HELP US

The United States was born in the spirit of science: What are we, if not a ***great experiment***?
We have kept our experiment ***viable*** by altering it through ***new laws*** and ***amendments*** to our Constitution, just as scientific theories change to reflect ***new knowledge***.

It should come as ***no surprise*** that many of the men who signed the Declaration of Independence had a ***profound*** interest in ***science.***
Benjamin Franklin was a brilliant experimentalist.
Benjamin Rush was an accomplished physician.
Thomas Jefferson had a voracious appetite for all things science, paleontology, astronomy, agricultural sciences, and mathematics.

As president, Jefferson would launch ***Meriwether Lewis*** and ***William Clark*** on a transcontinental expedition of ***discovery.***

Abraham Lincoln established the National Academy of Sciences.

Theodore Roosevelt pioneered modern conservation.

Franklin Roosevelt was the first president to appoint an official science advisor.
And ***John F. Kennedy*** set the United States on the path to the moon.

A scientific approach hasn't only shaped our government;
it has forged our economic might, as well.
We couldn't have built our mighty bridges, dams, and skyscrapers without science.
And when you look at the great innovators of American history, the vast majority were men and women who believed in the benefits of testing preconceived notions through experimentation.
That spirit led Andrew Carnegie to revolutionize the production of steel.
George Washington Carver to develop new crops—
—the Wright brothers to conquer flight—
—Henry Ford to pioneer the assembly line—
—and Steve Jobs to change the definition of the computer.
If we are to continue as a nation of prosperity, we need to encourage this spirit of ingenuity.

But science has *always* had to struggle against the forces of *superstition*.
So it would be a mistake to think that the *anti-science currents* we face today are entirely *new*.

Isaac Asimov wrote:
"The strain of anti-intellectualism has been a constant thread winding its way through our political and cultural life, nurtured by the false notion that democracy means that
'my ignorance is just as good as your knowledge.'"

It is what the comedian *Stephen Colbert* dubbed "*truthiness*," a feeling that an erroneous opinion that "sounds" true is just as valid as the *actual truth*.

But while these forces have *always* been present in American society, I have never seen them *infect* our national discourse as much as they do *now*.

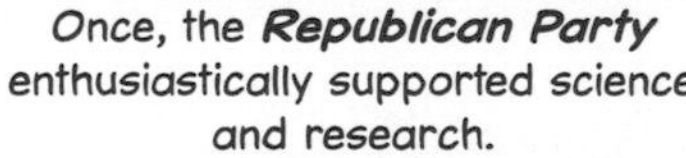
Sadly, science has become another political football in our bifurcated United States.
Once, the *Republican Party* enthusiastically supported science and research.

But recently many of its elected officials have *embraced truthiness* to guide their rhetoric and, even more damaging, their *policies*.
And lest we think this falls on only one side of the political divide, there is plenty of fearmongering among *Democrats* on issues such as *genetically modified organisms*.

There are ***many factors*** contributing to our current crisis:

the political ***divide***—

—a general ***loss of faith*** in experts and authority—

—and ***suspicion*** of corporations (such as Big Pharma and agribusiness).

Science has also had some ***self-inflicted*** wounds.

We have been told that chemicals like ***DDT*** are safe—

—seen ***unethical research*** like the Tuskegee Study ***exposed***—

RED MEAT?
GOOD?
BAD?

—and we are ***confused*** by shifting directives from scientists on our ***own health.***

The press has ***often failed*** in the way we have reported on scientific findings.

SCIENCE
BREAKTHROUGH

For starters, scientific issues are often ***complex*** and don't lend themselves to the simple ***sound bites*** of short news packages.

We've overhyped "medical breakthroughs," favored scientific ***self-promoters***, and focused on ***gee-whiz angles*** instead of educating the public.

But perhaps the biggest mistake the press makes is falling into false equivalence.
Not every scientific issue has two sides,
or certainly two equal sides.

And yet science "debates" are far too often reported in just such a manner.
A particularly damaging example of this phenomenon can be seen in irresponsible concerns over vaccine safety.

Immunizations have arguably saved ***more lives*** than any other scientific advance in human history.

And yet a few decades ago, ***charlatans***—led by a now-disgraced British doctor named ***Andrew Wakefield***—started to raise fears about the ***general safety*** of vaccines.

Wakefield claimed that vaccines could lead to autism, and even though his studies were highly flawed, he was given prominent press attention.
60
MINUTES

Dr. Wakefield was often pitted against ***reputable scientists*** who extolled the virtues and the safety of ***vaccines.***

But when you put two people on-screen and tell both "sides" of the story,
in the viewer's mind it immediately connotes fifty-fifty,
even if you say it doesn't.

The comedian ***John Oliver*** dramatically illustrated this point on the issue of ***climate change***—

—by bringing ***ninety-seven scientists*** onto the set of his HBO program to vividly ***demonstrate*** the fact that 97 percent of scientists believe human activities are leading to ***global warming***.

Needless to say, that is ***not*** how the issue has generally been covered.

It is incumbent on ***journalists*** and storytellers to handle science ***better***—
—a mission that has become a growing ***passion*** in this late chapter in my life.

I recently went to San Francisco for a meeting at the city's University of California campus (UCSF).
It is one of the best science and medical research centers in the world.
I toured the lab and met the students of Dr. Ron Vale, a world-renowned professor of cell biology.
While still a graduate student, he discovered an ingenious chemical machine—a type of protein—that carries material around your cells by walking along specialized tracks.
Vale continues to do cutting-edge research, but he has also taken on the mission of science communication with a level of passion that is inspiring.
When I visited Vale's lab, I was fascinated by how his team of thoughtful young researchers approached their work.

These women and men are ***explorers,*** as assuredly as ***Christopher Columbus*** and ***Neil Armstrong*** were.

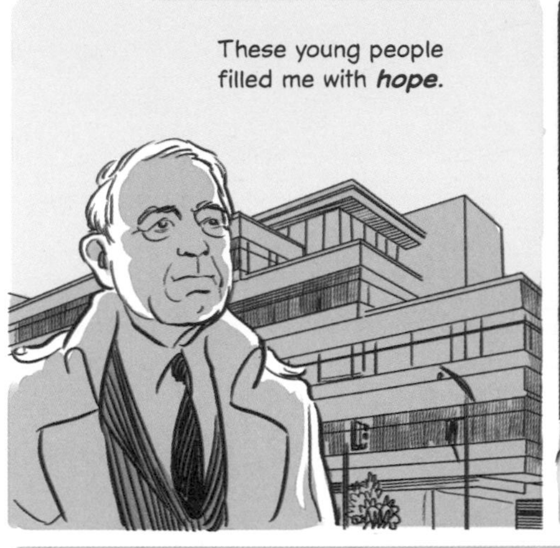
These young people filled me with ***hope.***

It is our job as citizens to make sure they are ***supported***, and my job as a journalist to effectively ***share their stories*** with the world.

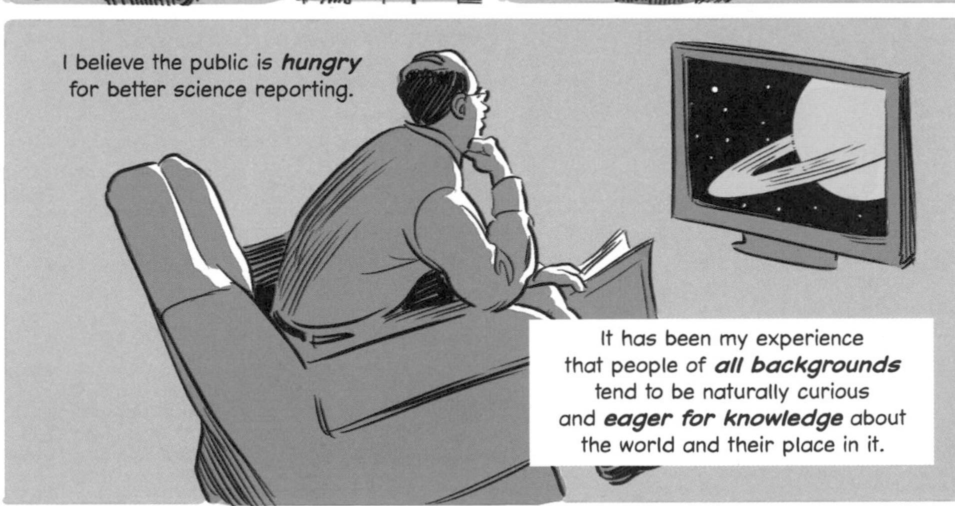
I believe the public is ***hungry*** for better science reporting.
It has been my experience that people of ***all backgrounds*** tend to be naturally curious and ***eager for knowledge*** about the world and their place in it.

Several years ago, I did a report on **neuroplasticity**, the ability of our brains to keep changing as we age.
We interviewed Nobel Prize-winning scientist **Eric Kandel**, who helped pioneer the field.
We also interviewed the **Dalai Lama**.
We learned that researchers studying **Buddhist monks** have discovered that their **deep meditations** actually **alter the structure** of their brains.
I received an **email** from a woman who worked in heavy construction in **Oklahoma**—not our **usual** target demographic for science reporting—she enthused:
"I always **knew** my mind could grow."

When I learn about scientific discoveries, I feel that ***my*** mind is growing ***also***, but this wasn't ***always*** the case.

In the era when I attended high school, ***esoteric knowledge*** about bacteria or the forces of physics was not perceived as a ***road*** to ***employment***.

Especially for blue-collar people like us.

In college, I took a ***chemistry*** class, and it was ***not*** a pleasant experience.

PERIODIC

My ***teacher*** was stiff and strict and I reasoned that science must also be a ***joyless pursuit***.

I faltered, and it was one of the few Cs I got in college.
When I took physics the following year, it wasn't much better.
REPORT CARD
A
B
C
Science courses scared me, so science scared me.

The *first time* the importance of science *really* struck me was back in the early 1960s.
I was working with producer David Buksbaum on the CBS News documentary investigating the tragedy of the *USS Thresher*—
—a *nuclear submarine* that was lost—with no survivors—during a deep-dive exercise off the coast of *Cape Cod* a year earlier.
I interviewed celebrated oceanographer *Roger Revelle* about the *physics* of the ocean depths.
No one *impressed* me as much as he did. There was an air of *exhilaration* in the lab.
It was a *world away* from my boring college science lectures.
This was what *science* was all about.
I saw a *vista* of *exploration* stretching out into the *future*. I left feeling more than intrigued. *I was inspired*.

I have heard many similar stories of students being ***turned off*** by science.

When I recently interviewed the British Nobel Prize-winning geneticist ***Sir Paul Nurse***—
—I was shocked to learn that he, too, had ***struggled*** in some of ***his*** introductory science classes in ***college***.

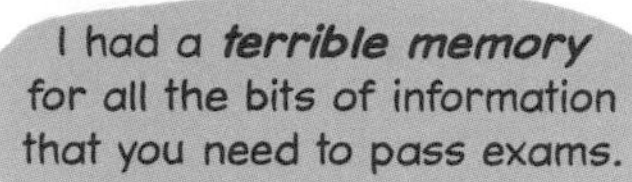
I had a ***terrible memory*** for all the bits of information that you need to pass exams.

Like me, he also had trouble with the ***periodic table***.

What really mattered to me—
—was understanding the ***basis*** and the ***order***. Then I could put names to it.
If I was just learning the names with no order, I was ***hopeless***.

When I asked Sir Paul how to ***inspire*** young minds, he said:
Do what ***I did*** when I was growing up.
Head out into the night and ***look up*** at the ***moon*** and ***stars***.

Wonder what it ***all means*** and you're already on the ***first step*** to science.

I fear *too many* of our young people are *bored or intimidated*—
—and thinking, like I did, that *somehow*—
—science is *not* for them.
Science is much more than an accumulation of *facts*—
—it is about a willingness to *reevaluate* our *assumptions* in the face of data to better see, understand, and *improve* our world.
These are values that have *shaped* the evolution of our modern *democracy*, so I think science can be a *bridge* that helps unite us as a nation.
If our *elected officials* turn their backs on this process, they will be *undermining* the forces that have *elevated our country*.

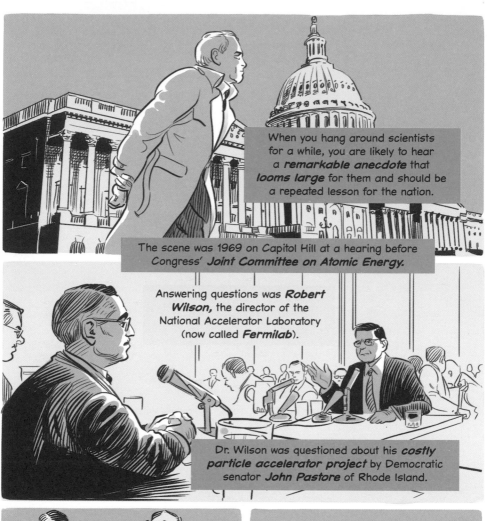

When you hang around scientists for a while, you are likely to hear a ***remarkable anecdote*** that ***looms large*** for them and should be a repeated lesson for the nation.

The scene was 1969 on Capitol Hill at a hearing before Congress' ***Joint Committee on Atomic Energy.***

Answering questions was ***Robert Wilson,*** the director of the National Accelerator Laboratory (now called ***Fermilab***).

Dr. Wilson was questioned about his ***costly particle accelerator project*** by Democratic senator ***John Pastore*** of Rhode Island.

Is there anything connected in the hopes of this accelerator that in ***any way*** involves the security of the country?

No, sir: I do ***not*** believe so.

Nothing at all?
Nothing at all.

It has no value in that respect?

It only has to do with the respect with which we regard one another, the dignity of men, our love of culture.
It has to do with these things. It has nothing to do with the military.
I am sorry.

Don't be sorry for it.
I am not, but I cannot in honesty say it has any such application.

Is there anything here that projects us in a position of being competitive with the Russians, with regard to this race?

Only from a long-range point of view, of a developing technology.
Otherwise, it has to do with: Are we good painters, good sculptors, great poets?
I mean all the things that we really venerate and honor in our country and are patriotic about.

In that sense, this new knowledge has all to do with honor and country, but it has nothing to do directly with defending our country except to help make it worth defending.

A country "worth defending"— how true.
And how elegant a plea for patriotism.
Science, like the arts, is about the most creative applications of the human mind.

We as a species have been able to figure out ***so much*** about ***life*** and the ***universe***—
—a process of discovery that is only ***accelerating***.
The fact that the United States has been a ***beacon*** for that progress should fill all Americans with ***pride***.
When the ***great histories*** of this nation are written centuries from now, I am ***confident*** that the role of ***science*** will occupy many chapters.
I ***desperately*** hope we can keep that narrative going and even ***growing***.
Our country's future place in the world ***depends*** *on that.*

Danny, show them your library card.

books

I was a young boy, on my first journey downtown to the main branch of the Houston Public Library.

It was the most spectacular building I had ever seen.

And I was being told I had a special key—

TREASURE ISLAND

—a library card that could unlock all the knowledge that surrounded me: the thousands of titles printed in the card catalog, the stacks that seemed to go on for miles.

I, the son of an oil field worker, now belonged here among the books. I dug in my pocket and produced my prized possession.

This experience was not unique.
In small farming towns and big industrial cities, in immigrant neighborhoods and in wealthy communities—
—people of all ages headed to libraries in large numbers to access a world of knowledge for free.
Hundreds of libraries had been built through the largesse of the industrialist Andrew Carnegie.
As a young man, Carnegie hadn't been able to afford a fee to the private library, and it was an experience he never forgot.

I recognize the ***quaintness*** in waxing nostalgic about libraries in ***an age*** when we have instantaneous access to more information than was contained in all the ***combined*** library collections of my ***youth.***

Still, libraries represent an aspirational notion of democracy.
They were, and ***still are,*** civic institutions that welcome ***anyone*** who wishes to become a more ***informed*** and independent citizen.

In books we can find expert and trustworthy ***scholarship*** on any subject imaginable.

By reading books, we can continually ***challenge*** our own biases and learn beyond our level of formal education.

These are qualities needed ***now*** more than ever.

Historically, leaders across the political spectrum have ***encouraged*** a reverence for knowledge.

A belief that our ***civic discourse*** should be infused with informed and ***well-reasoned*** arguments.

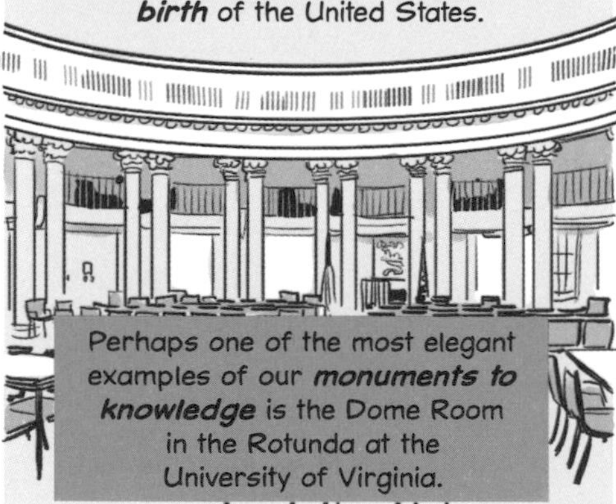
This has been a fundamental ***cornerstone*** of our democracy, stretching back to the ***birth*** of the United States.
Perhaps one of the most elegant examples of our ***monuments to knowledge*** is the Dome Room in the Rotunda at the University of Virginia.

This room, the building that houses it, and the University of Virginia itself were the creation of ***Thomas Jefferson,*** who championed ***freedom*** while owning slaves—thus embodying the contradictions into which our nation was born.

Jefferson's ***beloved library*** reminds us that ***reason*** and ***knowledge*** are ***necessary*** but ultimately ***insufficient*** for a ***moral government.***
PLATO
HORACE
MOLIERE
Jefferson modeled his Rotunda after the ***Pantheon*** in Rome, but whereas the original was built as a ***temple to the gods***—
—Jefferson created his as a ***place for scholarship.***
The term "***temple of learning***" is often used today as a metaphor, but that is ***literally*** what Jefferson conceived of for his library.

If you travel to Washington, D.C., you can see our country's debt to the power of books in the **very heart** of our federal city.
LIBRARY OF CONGRESS
SUPREME COURT
CAPITOL
I find the symbolism **inspiring:** three institutions that **write, judge,** and **archive** the words and thoughts that allow our nation to function.

The **Library of Congress** was founded in 1800, but the original collection was **lost** when the British burned Washington during the **War of 1812**.

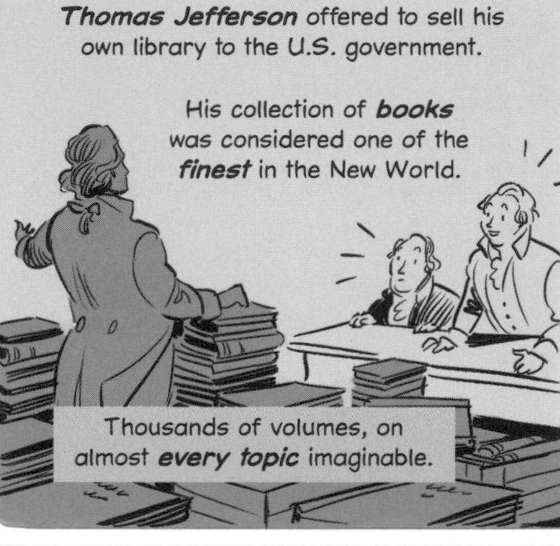
Thomas Jefferson offered to sell his own library to the U.S. government.
His collection of **books** was considered one of the **finest** in the New World.
Thousands of volumes, on almost **every topic** imaginable.

The library now had a bold new direction— a **reservoir** for capturing the world's **knowledge**.

America is justly proud of this gorgeous and palatial **monument** to its National sympathy and appreciation of Literature, Science, and Art.
It has been designed and executed entirely by **American art** and **American labor**— a fitting tribute for the **great thoughts** of generations past, present, and to be.

Growing up in working-class Houston, I had never heard of the **Library of Congress** or the grand Rotunda at the University of Virginia—
—but my local branch of the **Houston Public Library** showed me that books were not only important, they were also **objects of beauty**.
The stone building had **high ceilings**, big windows, and a red tile roof—
—its Italian-style **architecture** made the library seem worlds away from my hardscrabble neighborhood.
But while the library's physical charm was **impressive**, it was what was **inside** that made it **truly magical**.

And I had a wonderful guide, the librarian ***Jimmie May Hicks***—
—who served at the ***Heights branch*** library from the year of my birth, 1931, until her death in 1964.

Like all the best librarians, Ms. Hicks would ***suggest***, ***question***, and ***prod*** my reading—
—into new and ***unexpected*** directions.

The library now has a memorial plaque in her honor that reads, in part:
IN MEMORY OF
JIMMIE MAY HICKS
HOUSTON PUBLIC LIBRARY
"She dedicated her life to her profession and sought always to impart to others joy in acquiring knowledge and pleasure in the art of reading."

The importance of curated knowledge was ***encouraged*** at home, as well.
During my last year at elementary school, our principal called in all the ***parents*** to prepare them for the ***challenges*** of junior high.

My mother came back determined to get our family a set of encyclopedias.

This caused a bit of a disagreement.
This is a luxury we can't afford!

If we buy them on the installment plan, we can make it work.
Just having them in the house will help Danny!

It was a momentous day when they arrived at our doorstep.

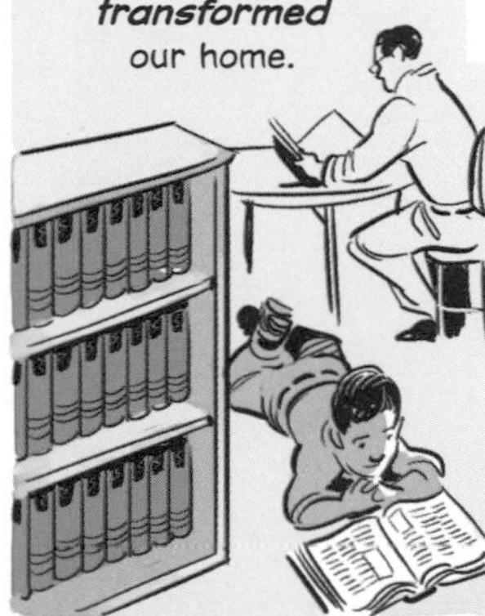
Just having those books on our shelves transformed our home.

Whenever any of us had a question, there was the promise of an answer, and an excuse for more learning.

My father's initial reluctance dissipated.
I can still see him rising from reading the newspaper to look up a name, location, or concept.

I kept that encyclopedia set well into my thirties.

We need to continue to teach our children how to **read**, not just to sound out words—
—but also to read **deeply and thoroughly**.

This must start **early** with the understanding that books are **important**.

I interviewed the music legend **Dolly Parton** a few years back—
—and her naturally **effervescent personality** really sparkled when we started talking about **books**.

Parton had grown up in the **poverty** of **Appalachia**.
She told me about her **father**, who had to **drop out** of school to work to **support** his family.

My daddy could not read nor write. Never had a chance to go to school. But my daddy was **so smart**.
You know, he was just—I've just always wondered what all my daddy **might have been** able to do had he had an education.

With him in **mind**, Parton founded a charity in 1995 to provide books to families in her home county of ***Sevier, Tennessee.***
Dolly Parton's IMAGINATION LIBRARY
The idea was **simple**: Families would receive age-appropriate books **every month** from when a child was **born** up until he or she turned **five**.
The program has grown **considerably**, first to communities across the state, then the United States, and now to countries **overseas**.
Today, more than **one million** children are enrolled and more than **eighty million books** have been shipped.
As Parton told me:
If you can **read**, you can educate **yourself**.
That was my **main** point.

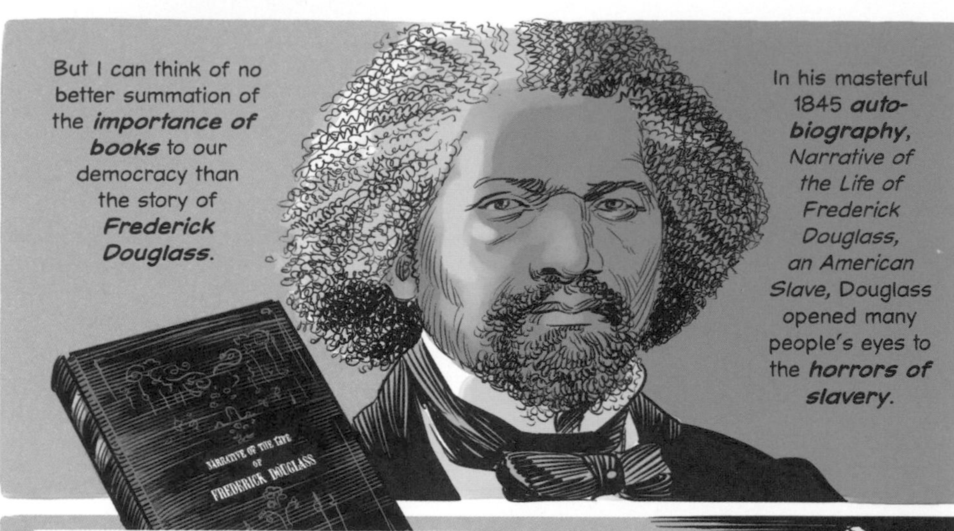
But I can think of no better summation of the *importance of books* to our democracy than the story of *Frederick Douglass*.
In his masterful 1845 *autobiography*, *Narrative of the Life of Frederick Douglass, an American Slave*, Douglass opened many people's eyes to the *horrors of slavery*.
NARRATIVE OF THE LIFE OF FREDERICK DOUGLASS

"Written by Himself." How could a man write so insightfully and be held in *bondage* to another?
Many reviewers at the time *noted* this contradiction.
Margaret Fuller, writing in the *New York Daily Tribune*, stated:
Considered merely as a narrative, we have never read one more simple, true, coherent, and warm with *genuine feeling*. It is an excellent piece of writing, and on that score to be *prized* as a specimen of the powers of the Black Race, which Prejudice *persists* in disputing.

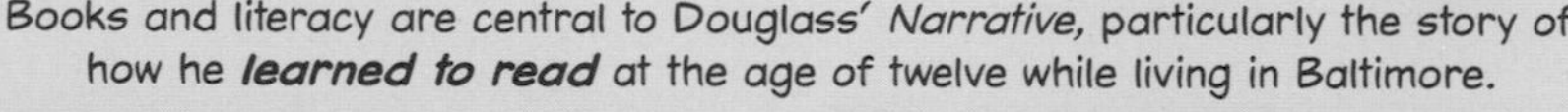
Books and literacy are central to Douglass' *Narrative*, particularly the story of how he *learned to read* at the age of twelve while living in Baltimore.

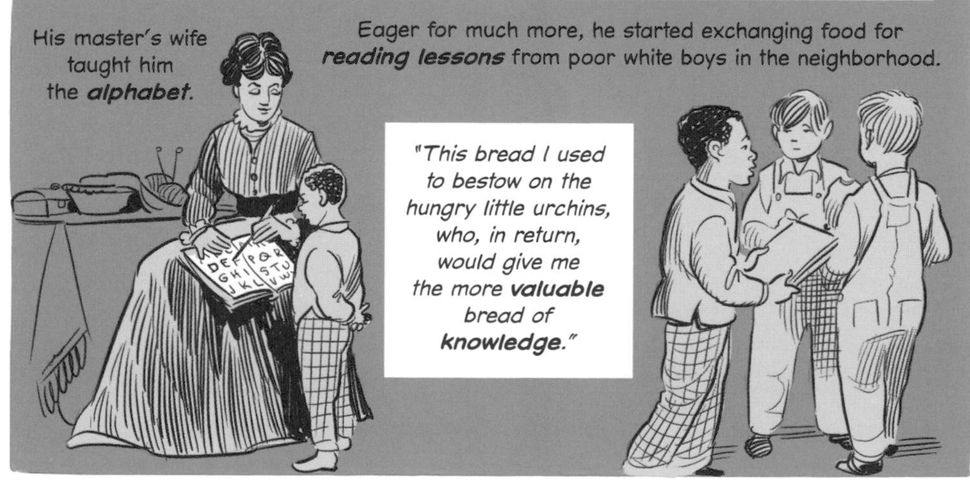
His master's wife taught him the *alphabet*.
Eager for much more, he started exchanging food for *reading lessons* from poor white boys in the neighborhood.
*"This bread I used to bestow on the hungry little urchins, who, in return, would give me the more **valuable** bread of **knowledge**."*
DEF GHI JKL
PQR STU VW

"I would at times feel that learning to read had been a curse rather than a blessing.
"It had given me a view of my wretched condition, without the remedy.
"It opened my eyes to the horrible pit, but to no ladder upon which to get out. In moments of agony, I envied my fellow slaves for their stupidity."
Douglass would eventually escape to the North and help change the fate of millions of enslaved people through the power of his words.
Today Douglass's papers are in the Library of Congress, the library started by the slaveholding Thomas Jefferson.
It strikes me as an act of poetic justice and a symbol of how the breadth of ideas we consider vital for our national identity has expanded.
We could not have made this journey without scholarship and thought, debate and self-reflection.
Democracy requires open access to ideas.
It requires a willingness to struggle and learn, to question our own suppositions and biases, to open ourselves as citizens, as a nation, to a world of books and thought.
Progress cannot be only intuited. It must be written, and read.

We find ourselves in a ***singular moment*** in our nation's history, where we have ***political leaders*** openly scornful of ***intellectualism*** and scholarship.

RESEARCH
STUDY
FACTS
We see many in power ***denigrate expertise*** and freely make up their own "***facts.***"

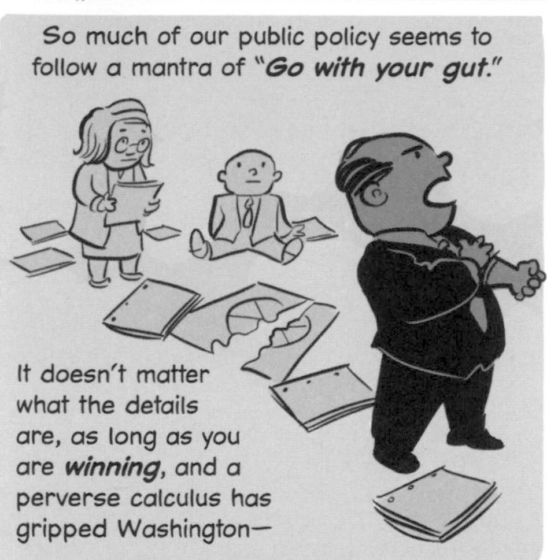
So much of our public policy seems to follow a mantra of "***Go with your gut.***"
It doesn't matter what the details are, as long as you are ***winning***, and a perverse calculus has gripped Washington—

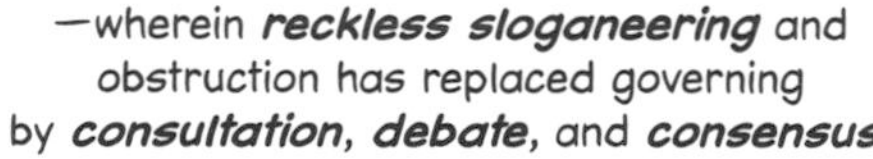
—wherein ***reckless sloganeering*** and obstruction has replaced governing by ***consultation***, ***debate***, and ***consensus***.

The ***scorn*** of knowledge (especially when the ***conclusions*** are painful) in exchange for ***fact-free rhetoric***—
—is not entirely new in our history, but it has always been the language of ***demagoguery***—

—and it is a ***betrayal*** of our traditions.

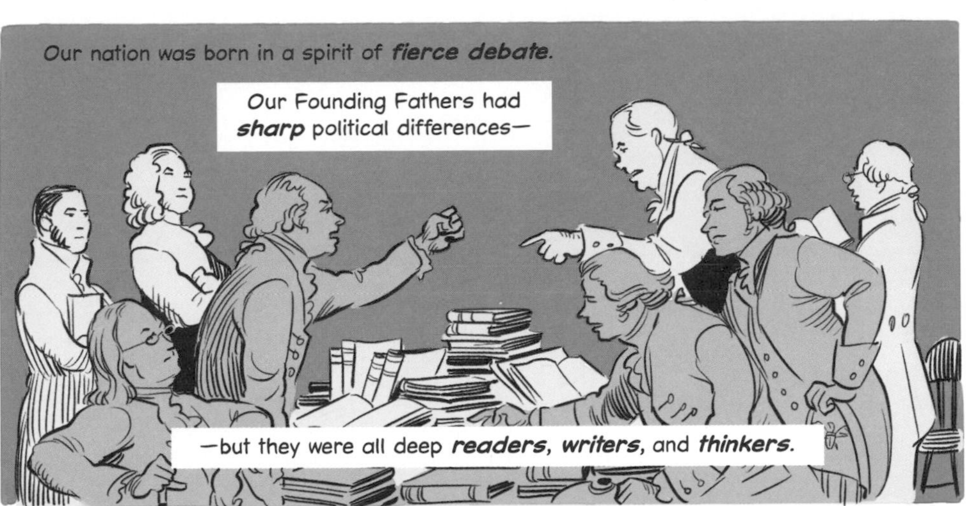
Our nation was born in a spirit of ***fierce debate.***
Our Founding Fathers had ***sharp*** political differences—
—but they were all deep ***readers, writers,*** and ***thinkers.***

When they set about to create a ***modern republic,*** they went into their ***libraries*** and pulled out the works of philosophers such as ***John Locke*** and ***Thomas Hobbes.***

They consulted the ***Greeks,*** the ***Romans,*** the philosophers of Europe, and the ***Bible.*** They revered the power of the ***written word*** and how it enabled a nation free from the whims of a king.

As ***John Adams*** wrote—

A republic is a government of ***laws,*** and not of ***men.***

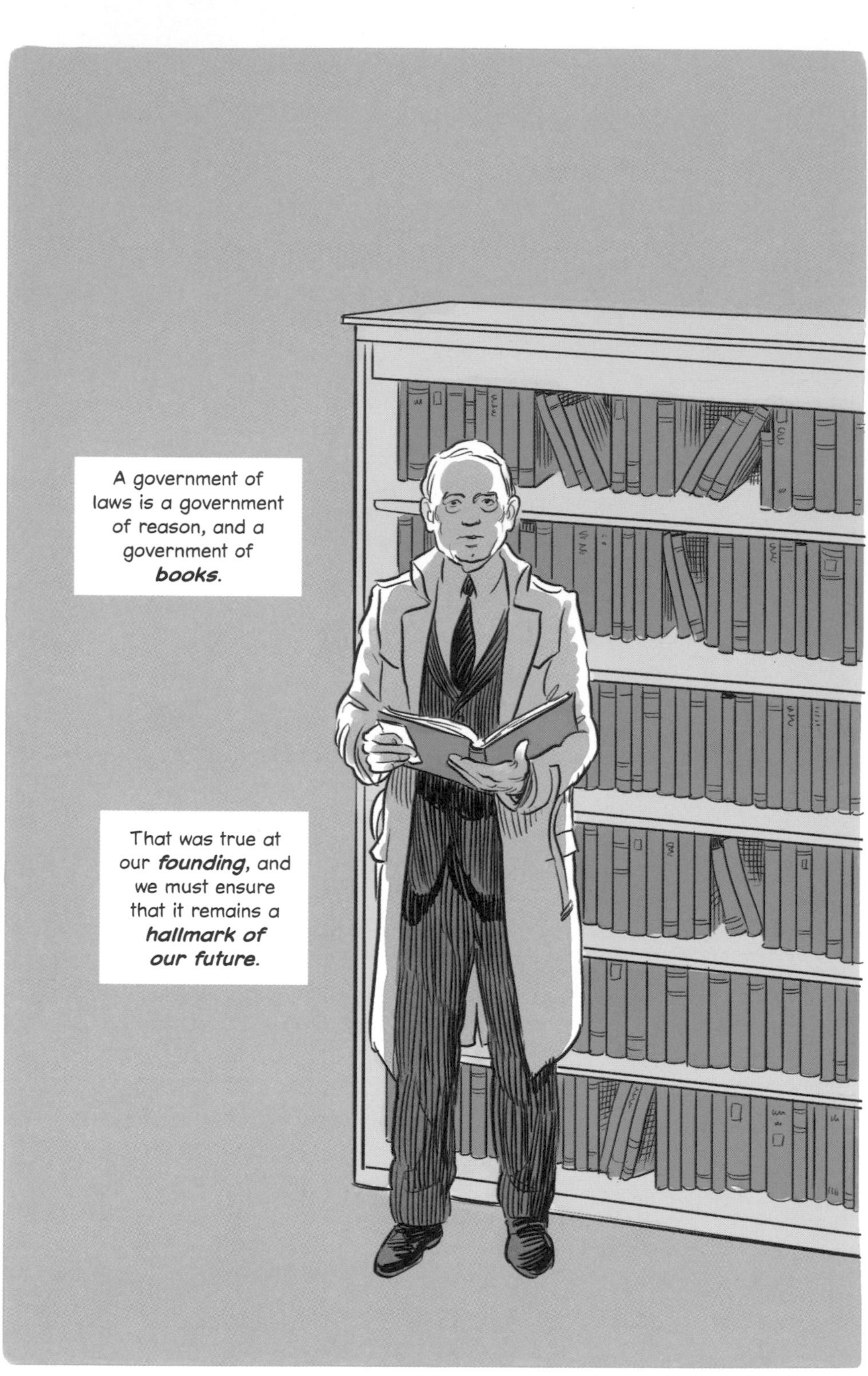
A government of laws is a government of reason, and a government of ***books***.
That was true at our ***founding***, and we must ensure that it remains a ***hallmark of our future***.

the arts
These days it is easier to occupy young minds with *mobile phones* and *tablet computers*—
—but I have *special respect* for the mothers and fathers who continue to lug around the bags of *crayons*, *markers*, and *paper*.
It brings a *smile* to my face when I see a child *drawing*.
I am encouraged when I see generations of the *future* engaging with the arts.
These pursuits are *central* to our American identity.
Patriotism can burst to the surface through many *geysers* of expression.

Perhaps one of the most ***inspiring*** visions for our nation can be found in a letter ***John Adams*** wrote to his wife, Abigail.

It was the spring of 1780, he was serving a ***diplomatic post*** in Paris, and the outcome of the Revolutionary War was ***still in doubt***.

But Adams had ***his eyes*** firmly set on the ***future***.

I must study politics and war that my sons may have liberty to study mathematicks and philosophy . . . in order to give their children a right to study painting, poetry, and musick.

It's an incredibly ***hopeful*** articulation of ***progress*** whereby the lasting ***worth*** of a nascent nation would depend on the ***arts*** being ***cultivated***, ***encouraged***, and ***appreciated***.

But there is another important ***current*** running through Adams' letter, a notion that ***American art*** would have to await further generations.

This sense of ***cultural inferiority*** would stretch well past the colonial era.

My first introduction to what might be considered art (at the time narrowly defined as high culture) came in high school.
But we weren't taught to celebrate the power of free expression in a vibrant American democracy.
ART
Instead, art was described to us mainly as a product of old world refinement and a necessary accoutrement for those of us intent on climbing the social ladder.

I now realize that my early ***lack of interest*** was also born of ***fear***.

I believed that ***understanding art*** was beyond my capabilities.

This way of thinking was ***common*** in mid-twentieth-century America.

Although the United States had just ***rescued*** Europe from the conflagration of ***fascism***—

—we still had a ***profound inferiority complex*** when it came to assessing our own ***cultural value***.

For many Americans, especially the ones I knew growing up, art felt elitist and far removed from our daily blue-collar lives.
Luckily for me, in more ways than one, that was about to change.

When I met **Jean,** we were in our early twenties and she had an enthusiastic ***thirst*** for the arts.
GALLER
509

I wanted to ***impress*** her, so on our second date I took her to the ***Alley Theatre.***
Alley
THEATRE

The play Jean and I saw that night was *The Glass Menagerie* by ***Tennessee Williams.***
I knew I wanted to accompany Jean on a ***lifetime of performances.***

When we relocated to the cultural mecca of ***New York***—
GALLERY
WARHOL
Campbells
—we witnessed the ***rise and fall*** of artistic fads and saw the first big shows of ***artists*** who went on to become ***household names.***

I also started to see art as an increasingly **democratic** enterprise.
I came to realize that the masterful lyrics of ***Hank Williams'*** *"I'm So Lonesome I Could Cry"* were much more than just a ***radio ballad***—
—they were ***American poetry***.
The silence of a falling star lights up a purple sky.
KANE
Artists may not swear an oath to ***serve*** in government or the military—
—but they swear an oath to ***freedom of expression*** that is no less worthy of recognition, especially in a democracy such as ***ours***.
Theirs are not always ***comfortable*** voices to hear, or even comfortable people to be around.
But they are the ***truth tellers*** whose works have challenged our national complacency.

Our art has been, like our country, boisterous and courageous and ***gloriously distinct***.
THIS MACHINE KILLS FASCISTS
It has expressed ***euphoria***, ***shame***, and ***outrage***.
It has been ***exalted*** and it has felt the sting of ***suppression and marginalization***.
It has been ***misunderstood***.
BELOVED
A NOVEL
TONI MORRISON
Perhaps most important, our art has been ***wonderfully diverse***.

Frank Lloyd Wright
Louis Armstrong
Georgia O'Keeffe
Ernest Hemingway
Johnny Cash
Charlie Chaplin
Andy Warhol
Mark Twain
Ella Fitzgerald
Jackson Pollock
Willie Nelson
Edward Hopper
Robin Williams
Carlos Santana
Martha Graham
Bob Dylan
George Gershwin
Langston Hughes
Ansel Adams
Maya Angelou
William Faulkner
Emily Dickinson
Martin Scorsese
Maria Tallchief
Marlon Brando
Stephen Sondheim
Elvis Presley
American art is ***proof*** that people from ***all*** backgrounds and corners of this country have something ***important*** to say.
Miles Davis
Willa Cather
Prince

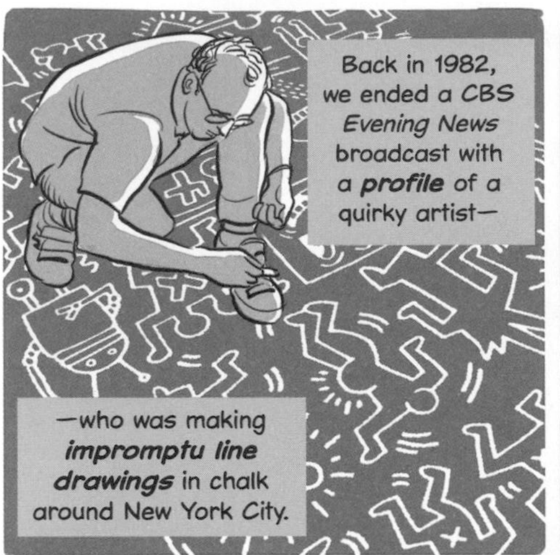
Back in 1982, we ended a CBS *Evening News* broadcast with a ***profile*** of a quirky artist—
—who was making ***impromptu line drawings*** in chalk around New York City.

I set it up with a bit of ***humor:***
One subway artist is making a name for himself somewhere besides the ***police blotter***.

He became one of our more famous pop artists. His name was ***Keith Haring***, and he was just a kid from Kutztown, Pennsylvania.
He felt that art should be accessible to ***everyone***.

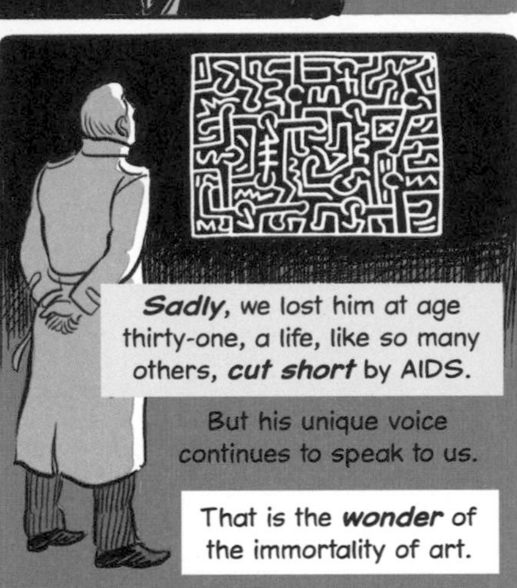
Sadly, we lost him at age thirty-one, a life, like so many others, ***cut short*** by AIDS.
But his unique voice continues to speak to us.
That is the ***wonder*** of the immortality of art.

Our Founding Fathers understood that ***free expression*** was central to democracy, a core value that separates us from ***autocratic and despotic societies*** where artists are often targeted as subversive and ***dangerous***.
In the spring of 2011, we were working on a report about ***government censorship*** in ***China*** when we interviewed one of the country's most famous contemporary artists, ***Ai Weiwei***.

Ai had already been the subject of harassments and even **severe beatings** at the hands of government authorities who were not **pleased** by his **art**.

He had become a fierce **critic** of the **corruption** that led to shoddily built schools that had **collapsed** during a major earthquake in 2008.
*Thousands of young students had been **crushed** to death.*

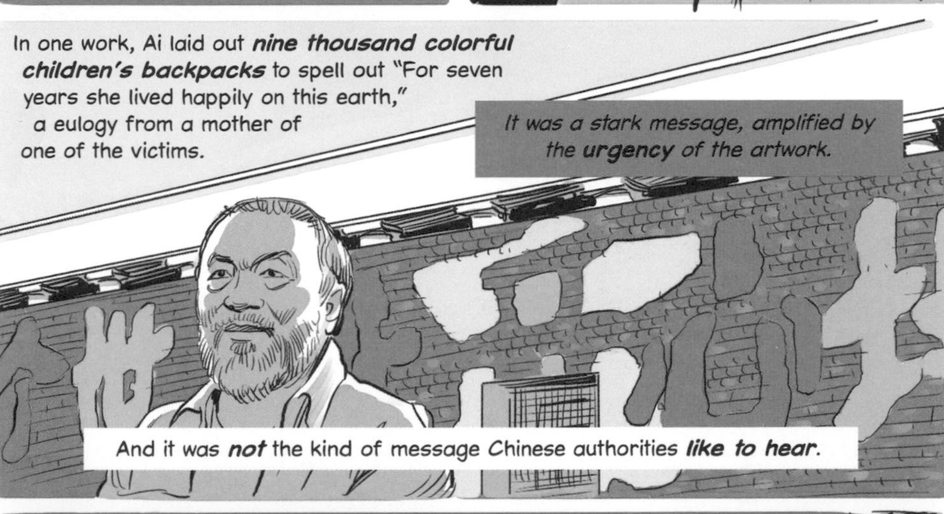
In one work, Ai laid out ***nine thousand colorful children's backpacks*** to spell out "For seven years she lived happily on this earth," a eulogy from a mother of one of the victims.
*It was a stark message, amplified by the **urgency** of the artwork.*
And it was ***not*** the kind of message Chinese authorities ***like to hear***.

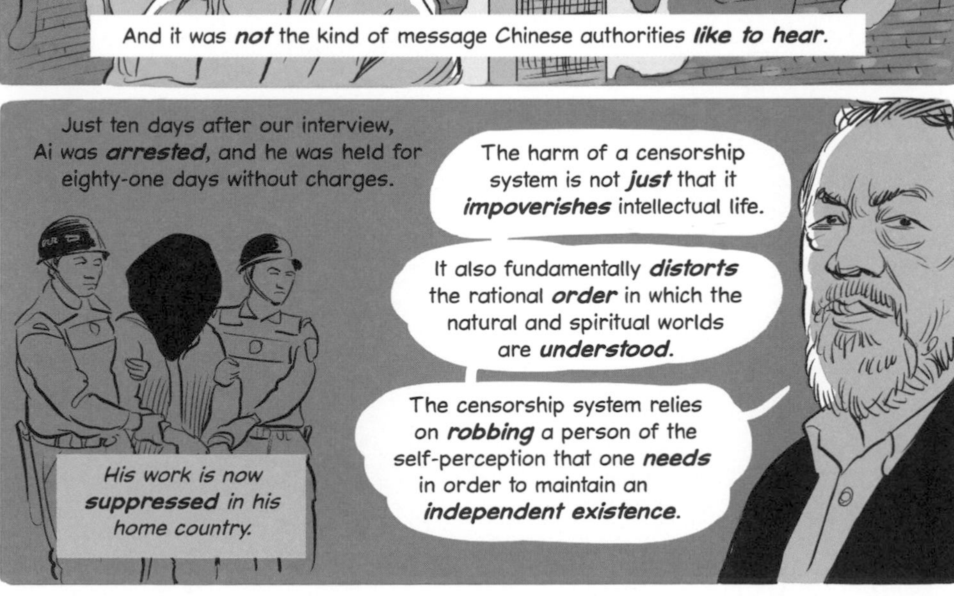
Just ten days after our interview, Ai was ***arrested***, and he was held for eighty-one days without charges.
The harm of a censorship system is not ***just*** that it ***impoverishes*** intellectual life.
It also fundamentally ***distorts*** the rational ***order*** in which the natural and spiritual worlds are ***understood***.
The censorship system relies on ***robbing*** a person of the self-perception that one ***needs*** in order to maintain an ***independent existence***.
*His work is now **suppressed** in his home country.*

The idea of art as "***access to independence*** and ***happiness***" is a notion that speaks to my own experience.

In ***art***, you can find voices that channel your ***own life story*** better than you could ever express it yourself.

And you can also find voices that introduce you to ***worlds*** you never would have otherwise visited.

In a diverse republic such as ours, both of these inspirations are especially ***important***.

One American artist whose work spoke to me with ***uncanny resonance*** was the greatly underappreciated playwright ***Horton Foote***.
He and I both were born in the same small Texas town of ***Wharton*** (although I moved to Houston when I was a year old), and we came to know each other after finding our ways to ***New York*** much later in life.

It is Foote's **original work** that stands out to me as a mark of greatness.
MAIN ST
5TH AV.
Foote's plays, screenplays, and memoirs are centered on an **America** that once was the norm but now has largely disappeared: **small-town, rural life**—
—where families intersected with one another countless times **across the generations.**
His work beats with the heart of a **democratic nation**, as he transformed the drama and comedy of **everyday life** into great art through his exquisite sense of **dialogue**.
Foote's plays remind me that some of the **best art** is the most **modest** in its framing and **far reaching** in its emotional impact.

—but I worry that his ***deceptively simple*** and superficially dated plays are perhaps falling ***out of favor***.

In art, as in our country more broadly, we cannot allow only the ***newest***, ***loudest***, and ***brashest*** voices to be heard.

While Foote always felt familiar, art also has a way of exposing you to a ***point of view*** you never could have imagined.

That is the case with one of my favorite singers—and, more important, songwriters: the country star ***Loretta Lynn***.

A coal miner's daughter who rose from poverty-stricken Appalachia to Nashville royalty, she epitomized the Horatio Alger stories and the American Dream—
—albeit with a very important twist.
Loretta Lynn achieved all this as a female artist.

Lynn's catalog of songs is one of the most *impressive collections* of socially relevant commentary in the history of American music.
As early as 1966, she was *challenging* her audience with a mournful story of a woman losing her husband to the *Vietnam War*. Entitled "Dear Uncle Sam"– it included poignant lyrics such as:
You said you really need him, but you don't need him like I do.
DECCA
DEAR UNCLE SAM
LORETTA LYNN
LORETT
DECCA
LORETTA LYNN
MCA RECORDS
THE PILL
LORETTA LYNN
She once told me about her songs being *banned:*
When they don't play 'em, you *know* it's gonna be a hit.
Many radio stations at the time *refused* to play "The Pill"—with lines like:
You've set this chicken your last time, 'cause now I've got the pill.
Lynn brought the intimate experiences of *working-class American women* to the nation's airwaves.
When I'd go to do a show, all the *women* would be out there. "*I'm with you,*" you know? And they'd *holler* at me and say, "You come to talk to *us women.*"
A lot of men *also* learned something from her songs, *this* one included.
I consider her another *patriotic artist*, a fearless *social commentator* channeling the experiences of an *overlooked* segment of society.

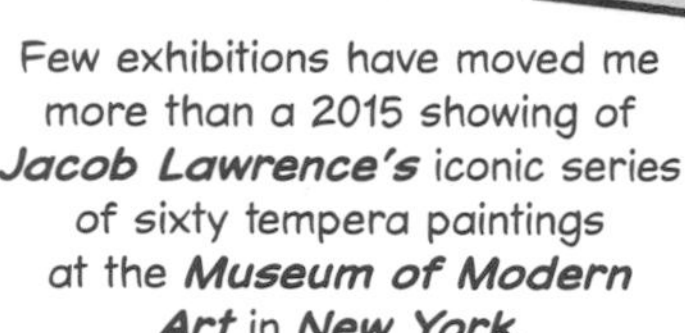

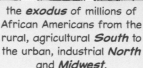

Produced over the course of 1940 and 1941, the series tells one of the truly *epochal transformations* of the American experience:
Few exhibitions have moved me more than a 2015 showing of *Jacob Lawrence's* iconic series of sixty tempera paintings at the *Museum of Modern Art* in *New York*.
the *exodus* of millions of African Americans from the rural, agricultural *South* to the urban, industrial *North* and *Midwest*.

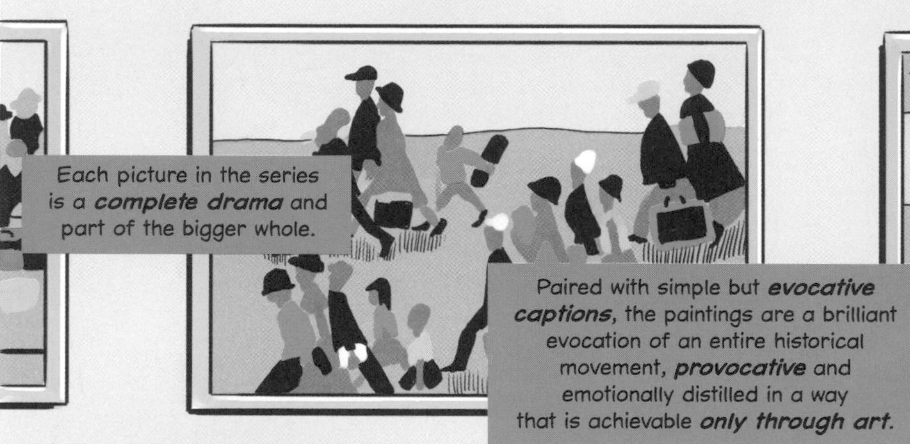

Each picture in the series is a *complete drama* and part of the bigger whole.
Paired with simple but *evocative captions*, the paintings are a brilliant evocation of an entire historical movement, *provocative* and emotionally distilled in a way that is achievable *only through art*.

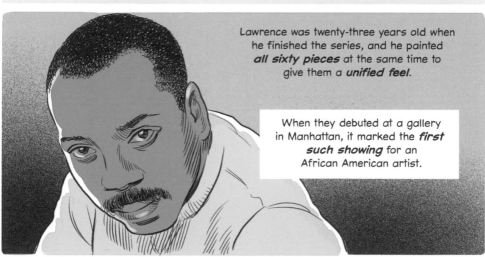

Lawrence was twenty-three years old when he finished the series, and he painted *all sixty pieces* at the same time to give them a *unified feel*.
When they debuted at a gallery in Manhattan, it marked the *first such showing* for an African American artist.

Lawrence was living in New York in the midst of the Harlem Renaissance, and one need not be a scholar to see the cross-currents of influences in the work.
APOLLO
TORIA
HARLEM
Lawrence's art was placed alongside photographs and journalism that had inspired him.

There was a film of the great Marian Anderson singing "My Country, 'Tis of Thee."

For me, the most effective accompaniment to Lawrence's work in the show was film of Billie Holiday singing "Strange Fruit."
Southern trees bear a strange fruit
Blood on the leaves and blood at the root

The word "lynching" is never mentioned in the song, but the terror and horror of the act is palpable.

Similarly, Lawrence addresses lynching in a pair of paintings in his series, but *neither* shows a dead body.

Taking in Lawrence's paintings and the song "Strange Fruit," I was struck by the *power of art* to move me.

I was *curious* about the story behind "Strange Fruit," and I was in for a *surprise*.

It was written by *Abel Meeropol*, a child of Jewish immigrants who taught at a public high school in the Bronx.

He had seen a photograph of a *lynching victim* that he couldn't get out of his mind, and he turned it into a poem, then put it to music.

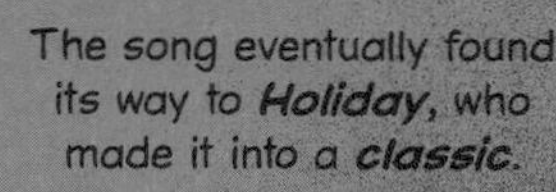

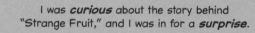

The song eventually found its way to *Holiday*, who made it into a *classic*.

In 1999, *Time* magazine dubbed it the *song of the century*.

Art is an attempt to capture the truths of the world as you see it in a ***medium*** you can ***share with others.***

It is about lending your ***voice,*** your perspective, to local, national, and global ***conversations.***

And that is ***why,*** in the United States in particular, our definition of ***what is art*** and who is an artist must be as varied as our citizenry.

I am relieved that we have escaped the ***narrow definitions*** of art from my childhood, a development gloriously celebrated in the musical ***Hamilton.***

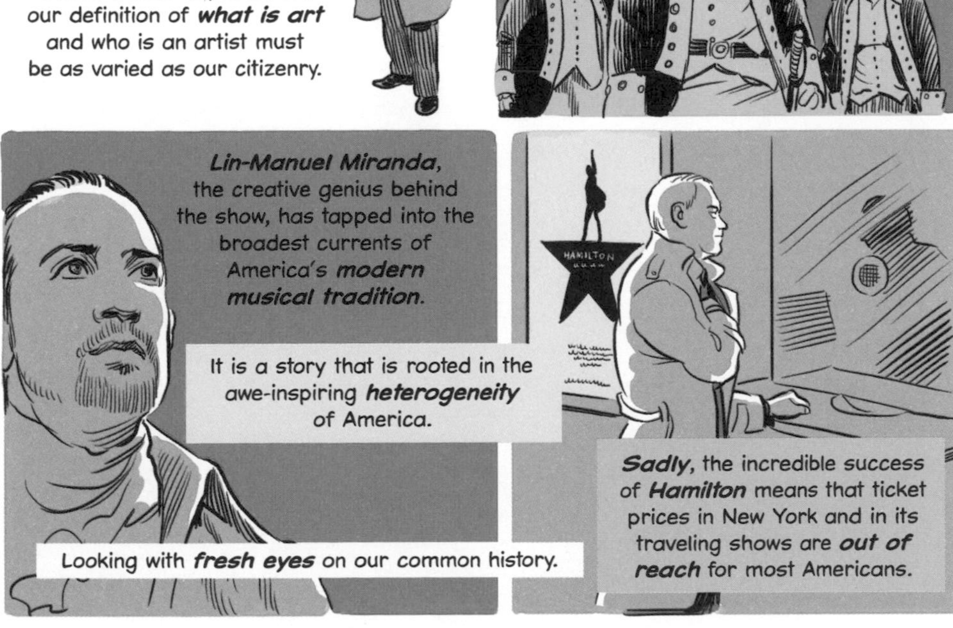
Lin-Manuel Miranda, the creative genius behind the show, has tapped into the broadest currents of America's ***modern musical tradition.***
It is a story that is rooted in the awe-inspiring ***heterogeneity*** of America.
Looking with ***fresh eyes*** on our common history.
HAMILTON
Sadly, the incredible success of ***Hamilton*** means that ticket prices in New York and in its traveling shows are ***out of reach*** for most Americans.

Great art like this should be accessible to not *only* the rich and well connected, but to *everyone*.
Our art is *our story*. It *grows* with the *inclusion* of different people and cultures, and we are *stronger* for it.

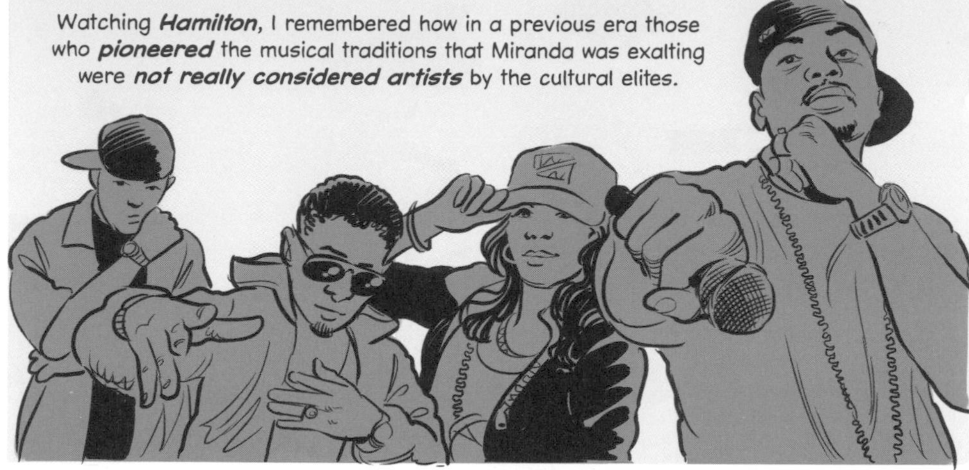
Watching *Hamilton*, I remembered how in a previous era those who *pioneered* the musical traditions that Miranda was exalting were *not really considered artists* by the cultural elites.

And there was a time, not so long ago, when these *young, beautiful, diverse actors* and *musicians* would be told that their voices were *not worthy* of inclusion on Broadway stages or in concert halls.

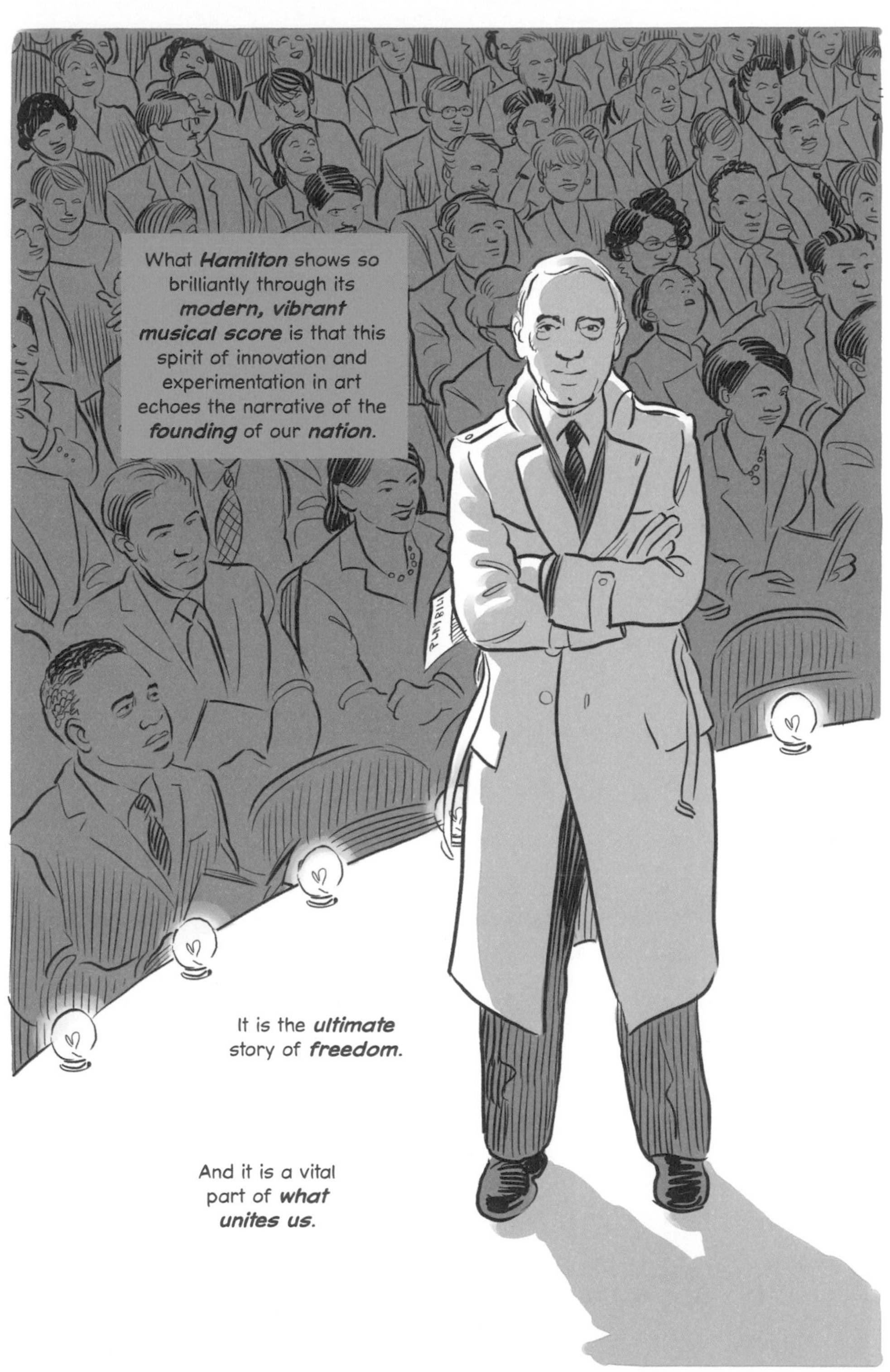
What *Hamilton* shows so brilliantly through its ***modern, vibrant musical score*** is that this spirit of innovation and experimentation in art echoes the narrative of the ***founding*** of our ***nation***.
PLAYBILL
It is the ***ultimate*** story of ***freedom***.
And it is a vital part of ***what unites us***.

5

responsibility

the environment

This picture is considered one of the most ***iconic images*** in human history.

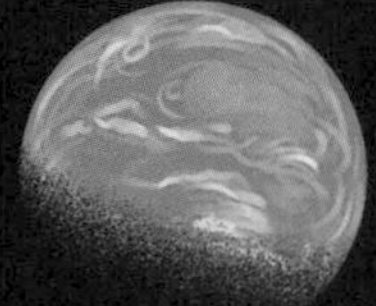

It altered our sense of ourselves as a species and the place we call ***home***.

The photograph has a name: ***Earthrise***.

The image was captured by astronaut ***William Anders*** of *Apollo 8* on the first manned mission to orbit the ***lunar sphere***—

—and the photograph can be seen as a ***mirror image*** for every vision humans had ever experienced up to that point.

From before the dawn of history, our ancestors looked up in the ***night sky*** and saw a brilliant ***moon***, often in shadow.

But in that moment on *Apollo 8,* three men from our planet looked back and saw ***all the rest of us*** on a small disk with oceans, clouds, and continents.

This image, so peaceful and yet so ***breathtaking***, was taken at the end of a turbulent year.

It was Christmas Eve 1968, but from up there you would never know that a ***hot war*** was raging in Vietnam or that a ***Cold War*** was dividing Europe.

You wouldn't know of the ***assassinations*** of Dr. Martin Luther King Jr. or Bobby Kennedy.

From that ***distance***, people are invisible, and so are ***cities, countries***, and ***national boundaries***.

All that separates us ethnically, culturally, politically, and spiritually is ***absent*** from the image. What we see is ***one fragile planet*** making its way across the vastness of space.

The photograph is widely credited with galvanizing a ***movement*** to protect our planet.

The 1960s and '70s were times of such social upheaval that the ***environmental movement*** is often overlooked.

But real action was happening.

In 1962, ***Rachel Carson***, a marine biologist, published one of the most important books in American history, *Silent Spring*.

SILENT SPRING Rachel Carson

It focused on the dangers of synthetic pesticides like ***DDT***, showing how these chemicals could insidiously enter an ecosystem and wreak unintended ***havoc*** on the health of a wide range of animals, including ***humans***.

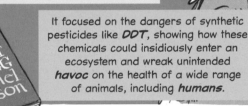

The book hit like a ***thunderclap***.

The reaction from the chemical industry was ***fierce*** and unrelenting, but the public uproar was even more ***substantial***.

The moral weight of Carson's argument changed the equation for how we measured our ***actions;***

the ***health*** of the ***earth*** became part of the discussion.

SAVE
BAN
EXTINCT

The book contributed to the rising pressure on government officials to act to ***protect the planet***.

EARTH DAY
IL 22
EPA
CLEAN WATER ACT
The environment was now an important ***national priority***—
—and ***support*** for it was ***bipartisan.***
There was a belief at the time that ***environmentalism*** was a series of ***local battles.***
Over time, we saw environmental threats become more regional, with ***acid rain*** and the ***depletion*** of the ***ozone layer.***
It was hard to imagine, though, that we could harm the planet on a ***global scale.***
But all the while, ever since the start of the industrial revolution, an ***odorless and invisible pollutant*** was being pumped into our atmosphere with increasing volume.
We now know that ***carbon dioxide*** and the resulting climate change is a threat of a magnitude ***unlike anything*** we have ever seen before.

In the summer of 2007, I traveled 450 miles north of the ***Arctic Circle***—

—to the ***Canadian tundra*** to report on a development that was ***shocking*** for any student of history.

For centuries, famed explorers had searched for a ***shipping route*** from ***Europe*** to ***Asia*** through the ***frigid north***—

It was dubbed the ***Northwest Passage,*** and it proved to be a deadly and illusory dream—

—as many ships and men went in to ***never return***.

So when my colleagues and I had heard reports that the melting sea ice was possibly ***unlocking the passage,*** we set about to document the dramatic climate change at the end of the earth.

What both the scientists and the ***local inhabitants*** understood was that—

—a world of ice was undergoing rapid and ***unpredictable*** change.

Even in the summer, it had once been largely ice.
The seal pelts are not as thick because of the warmer weather—
—and our people's way of life is in danger of being lost.

It was an awesome realization that Earth, which has always seemed **boundless**, is so susceptible to the negative by-products of human activity.
Perhaps that is what makes it so difficult for some to **accept** climate change.

As we walk through nature, it seems so robust and **permanent**.

And for the vast majority of the history of our species, we did not have the **power** to **destroy** the planet.

But if you look back to the beginning of the environmental movement, you will see that it sprang from a dawning realization of how **damaging** humans could be.
In the late nineteeth century, the mighty **bison** of the American West, estimated to once have numbered in the **tens of millions**—

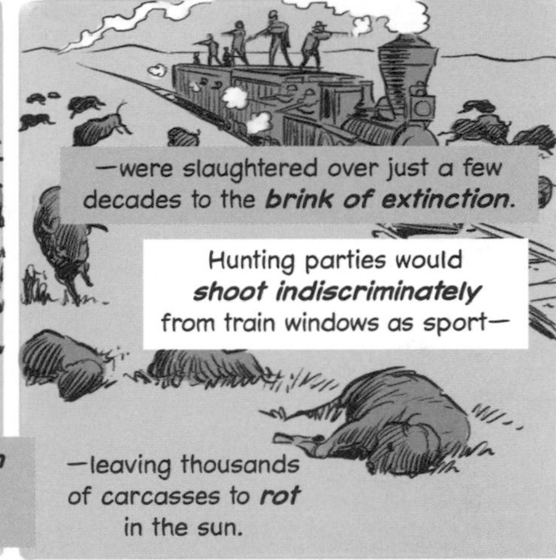
—were slaughtered over just a few decades to the **brink of extinction**.
Hunting parties would **shoot indiscriminately** from train windows as sport—
—leaving thousands of carcasses to **rot** in the sun.

A seemingly limitless resource suddenly was on the **verge** of **disappearing**.
By then, a growing spirit of **naturalism** was capturing the nation's attention—
—personified by writers like **Henry David Thoreau**.

And leading citizens in the United States, men with political power like **Theodore Roosevelt**, decided to act.
They formed **conservation clubs** that began to have an effect on the federal government.

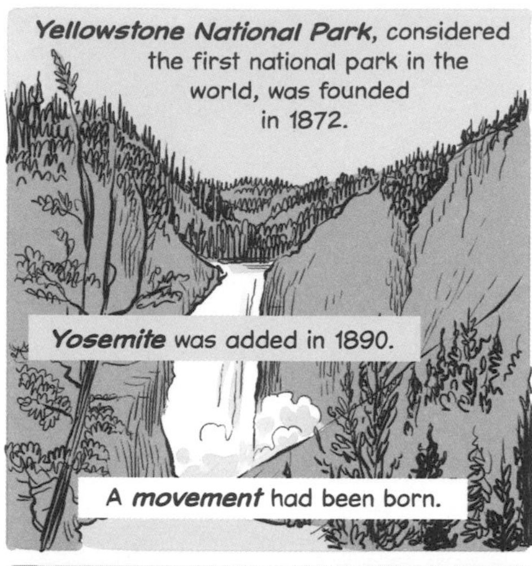
Yellowstone National Park, considered the first national park in the world, was founded in 1872.
Yosemite was added in 1890.
A ***movement*** had been born.

But meanwhile, a very ***different revolution*** had begun half a world away.

The first modern ***internal combustion engine*** was built in the 1870s.

In 1886, German engineer ***Karl Benz*** patented the first ***motorcar***.

Over the ensuing century and decades, as the ***environmental movement*** grew in its scope and importance, Earth was getting ***sicker***.

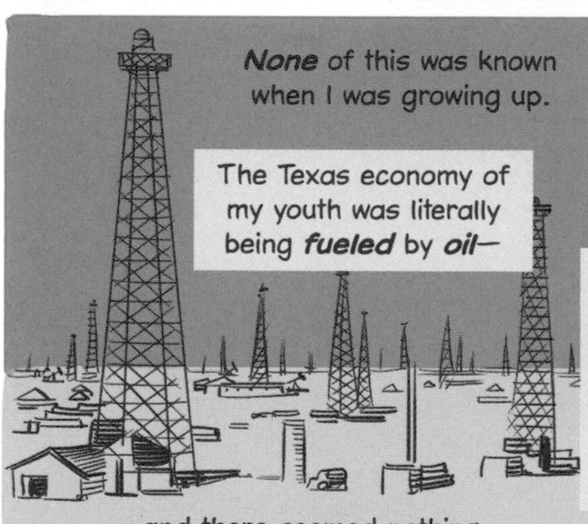
None of this was known when I was growing up.
The Texas economy of my youth was literally being ***fueled*** by ***oil***—

—and there seemed nothing incompatible with ***black gold*** and the health of the wide world outside my door.

Some of my ***earliest memories*** were of running through the ***wild meadow*** that bordered my neighborhood on the outskirts of Houston, looking at ***bugs***, ***lizards***, and, it being Texas, a lot of ***snakes***.

There was a ***creek*** a little farther out, and when I was young, my mother made it known to me that it was a boundary I ***dare not cross***.

Beyond the creek lay deep woods, and as I grew older, I was allowed to wander alone beneath the ***strong oaks*** and towering pines, turned loose in ***nature***.

In the midst of the woods was the ***Buffalo Bayou***, and I learned how to swim in its languid waters.

In truth, the bayou had already been polluted by the ***oil refineries*** and ***chemical plants*** around Houston. But we boys, frolicking in the water, didn't know that.

We were living out our fantasies of being latter-day ***Tom Sawyers*** and ***Huck Finns***.

In that great meadow and the forest beyond, the world seemed ***exciting and alive.***
My father was the kind of hunter who ***believed*** that you shouldn't hunt something you didn't know a lot about—
—and he instilled in me a ***deep respect*** for the natural world.
My father also believed that you ***ate*** what you killed, and so my mother had a number of recipes that fit both ***rabbit*** and ***squirrel*** interchangeably.
It may not sound like much, but it was ***pretty good.***
My father would also usually get a couple of ***deer*** during the hunting season, which was the legal limit.
We would eat every bit that was edible, and that could take ***quite a while.***
Dad was terrific with a shotgun, so we spent many a time cleaning, then eating, ***ducks*** and ***quail.***

Going into the forest with my dad was a backdrop to my young life.
It was just what people did.
I was expected to be able to identify the species of trees and to know how to avoid getting lost.
Nature wasn't something that you drove to, or planned on seeing, or for which you bought a fancy outdoor wardrobe.
51
Today most of us encounter few animals and plants in our daily lives.
—and most of what we do see are either the ones we have domesticated or the vermin and weeds that can thrive in the cracks of modernity.
Now most of us can see only a few faint stars at night, the ones bright enough to make it through the domes of light that enclose our metropolises.
Thirty percent of the people on the planet can't even see the Milky Way.

We as a nation have done much to ***exploit*** the land, ***despoil*** it, and ***pollute*** it.
From wildlife to wildfires, we have been ***shortsighted*** in our management.

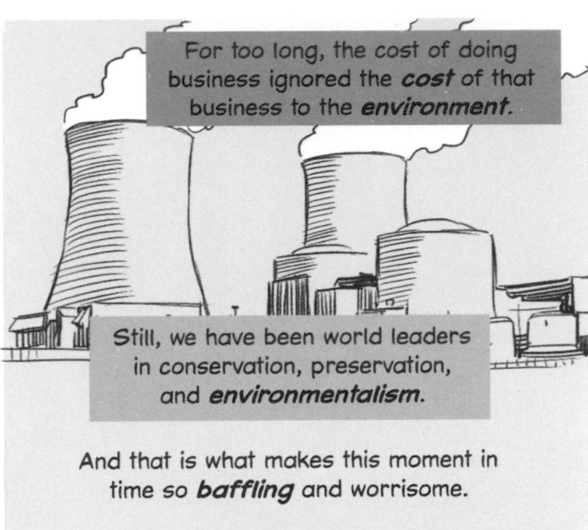
For too long, the cost of doing business ignored the ***cost*** of that business to the ***environment***.
Still, we have been world leaders in conservation, preservation, and ***environmentalism***.
And that is what makes this moment in time so ***baffling*** and worrisome.

Somehow the environment has become yet another ***point*** of ***contention*** between ***Democrats*** and ***Republicans***.
It is striking that those who live in urban centers tend to vote for ***Democratic candidates*** who mostly favor stricter environmental regulations.
OTE

Meanwhile, those in rural areas tend to vote for ***Republican candidates*** who more often advocate for laxer oversight of land, water, and pollution.
JONES
REPUBLICAN

But whatever the cause, it is important to note that these ***political and social divides*** over the environment were not always this way.

It was an ***odd experience*** watching the heated debate—
—as a cap and trade bill for carbon dioxide emissions and climate change made its way through Congress in ***2009***.

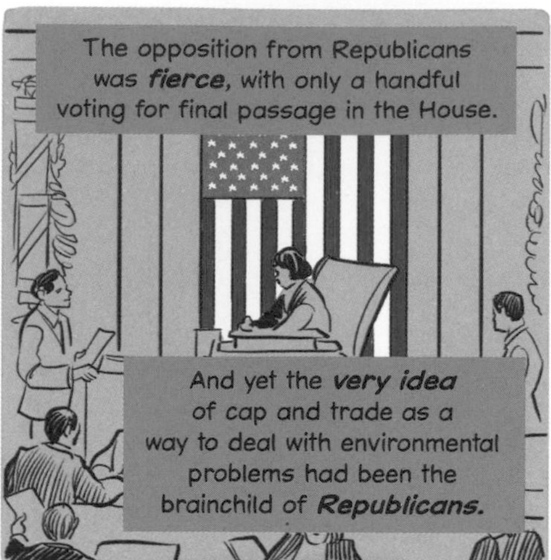
The opposition from Republicans was **fierce**, with only a handful voting for final passage in the House.
And yet the **very idea** of cap and trade as a way to deal with environmental problems had been the brainchild of **Republicans.**

When I sat down recently with **George Shultz**—
—he spoke with pride of the **Republican legacy** on the environment.
Secretary Schultz had become a vocal advocate for protecting the planet against **climate change.**

He reminded me that:
Major environmental **progress**—

—from **the founding of the EPA** to tackling the ozone and acid rain problems, to strengthening clean water and air acts—
happened under **Republican administrations**.

Questions of the environment boil down to **acts of leadership**.
We need a **balanced** approach.

We will never return to some **mythic state** of environmental **purity**.
Nor would we **want** to.
But that doesn't mean we can't be **wiser** about how we use our **limited resources** and protect our planet.

We humans seem to have a hard time **measuring risk.**
We can see the dangers in the **moment**—

—but threats that stretch over the **course of generations** are hard for us to judge, let alone **act to remedy.**
Climate change is just such a problem.

Even though we already see very **worrisome** fluctuations in Earth's functions—

—the most **dire effects** will not strike with full force until well after I am gone.
We can hide from the truth for now, but it will not **last.**

In my interview with **Secretary Shultz,** he described climate change as a **clear and present danger** even if many of his fellow Republicans did not see it that way.
Those who deny climate change now will ultimately be "**mugged by reality.**"
It is a strong phrase. The danger is that when the climate deniers are finally **mugged,** it will be, by definition, too late.

Often I find myself thinking back to my boyhood out in the forests and meadows—
—and how those experiences spurred in me a love of our natural world.
My eyes focused on the action in the stream, I'd glance up and begin singing slowly.
Just like a tree planted by the water, I shall not be moved. I shall not, I shall not be moved.
The hymn may say I shall not be moved, but I often am, in that strange and mystical way engaging in nature often moves us.
There is an elegance to birches.
I've always liked them because my long-departed mother loved them so. Born, raised, and buried on the semitropical Texas Gulf Coast, she never saw a live birch, only pictures in a book.
Mother's favorite tree, however, was the native magnolia, which flourishes all along the Texas Gulf Coast and adjacent piney woods.
She loved their strength and the fragrance of their large white blossoms. The scent permeating and enveloping in the heavy humidity of Texas nights is among the fondest memories of my childhood.
I like to sit out there on the river for a long while and take a deep breath and close my eyes. Nature doesn't please only our sense of sight.
Nature has the power to inspire one's mind and move one's soul like great music or poetry.
It can fill you with humility when you encounter the otherworldliness of the Grand Canyon.
It can fill you with awe when you tilt your head back and try to tease out the top of a towering redwood.
And it can fill you with sadness when you see how much the glaciers in Glacier National Park are receding.
What are we doing? What have we done?

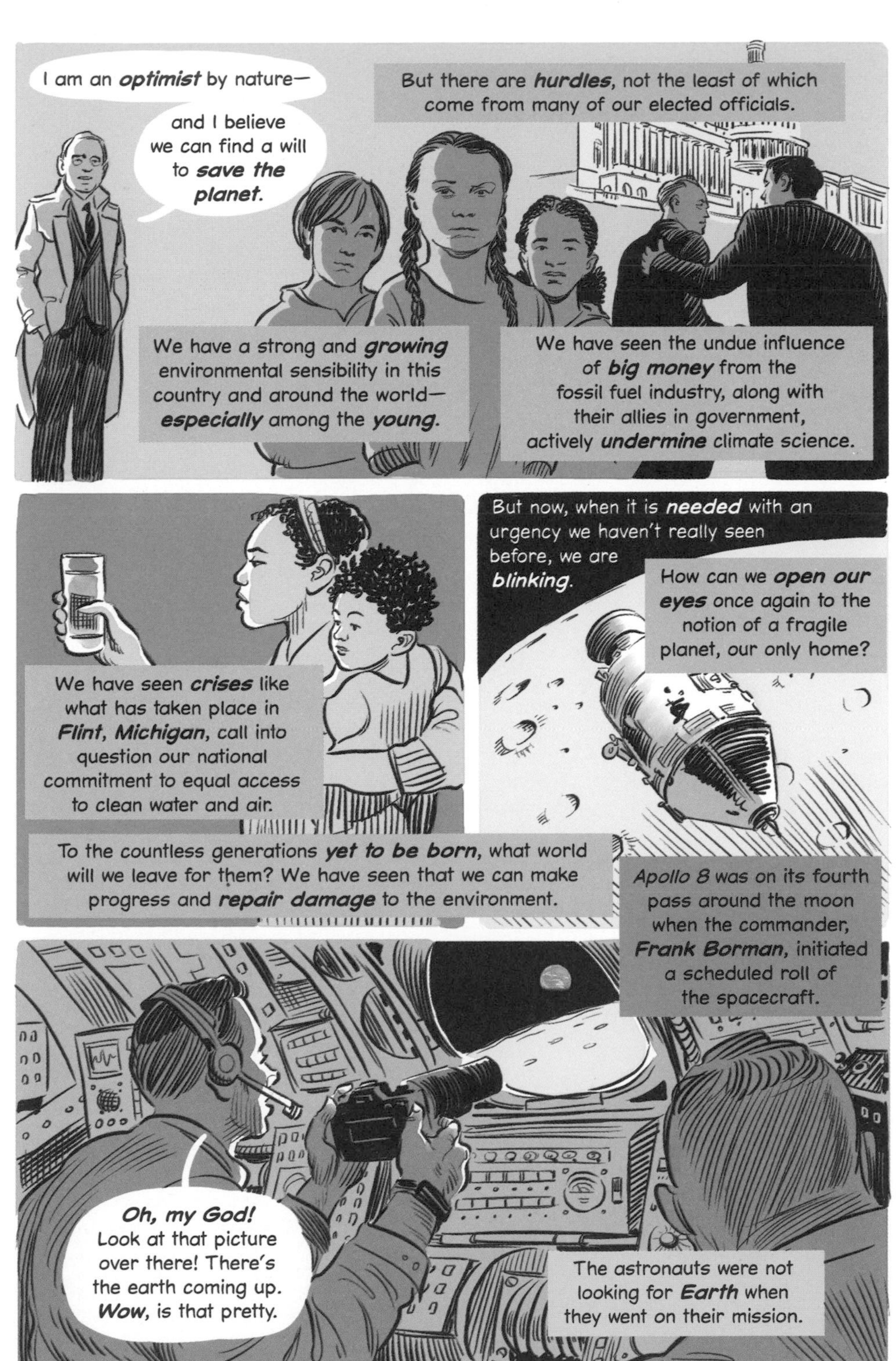
I am an optimist by nature—
and I believe we can find a will to save the planet.
But there are hurdles, not the least of which come from many of our elected officials.
We have a strong and growing environmental sensibility in this country and around the world—especially among the young.
We have seen the undue influence of big money from the fossil fuel industry, along with their allies in government, actively undermine climate science.
We have seen crises like what has taken place in Flint, Michigan, call into question our national commitment to equal access to clean water and air.
But now, when it is needed with an urgency we haven't really seen before, we are blinking.
How can we open our eyes once again to the notion of a fragile planet, our only home?
To the countless generations yet to be born, what world will we leave for them? We have seen that we can make progress and repair damage to the environment.
Apollo 8 was on its fourth pass around the moon when the commander, Frank Borman, initiated a scheduled roll of the spacecraft.
Oh, my God! Look at that picture over there! There's the earth coming up. Wow, is that pretty.
The astronauts were not looking for Earth when they went on their mission.

The space historian Andrew Chaikin said Anders told him later,
"We were trained to go to the moon. We were focused on the moon, observing the moon, studying the moon, and the Earth was not really in our thoughts until it popped up above the horizon."
We need this vision of a unified and cohesive Earth to pop up once again over the horizon of our global complacency.
We need to consider, with awe and humility, the future of our fragile home.

public education
Aa Bb Cc Dd Ee Ff Gg Hh Ii Jj
4 + 3 =
When I entered first grade in 1937, Texas was still ***mostly rural***, and Houston was a far cry from the sprawling ***metropolis*** it is today.
William G. Love Elementary School was in one of the ***poorer*** sections of town, but it was rich in ***leadership*** and dedicated, ***talented*** teachers.
All of them were ***women***.
In that period, with few exceptions, the ***only work*** outside the home open to a ***woman***—
—was as a nurse, a secretary, a waitress, or a ***teacher***.
And teaching was an option for only the comparatively few women who had ***finished college***.
So it is ***no wonder*** that Love Elementary, in the heart of "the wrong part of town," was loaded not just with ***women***—
—but with very ***smart***, ***hardworking*** women.

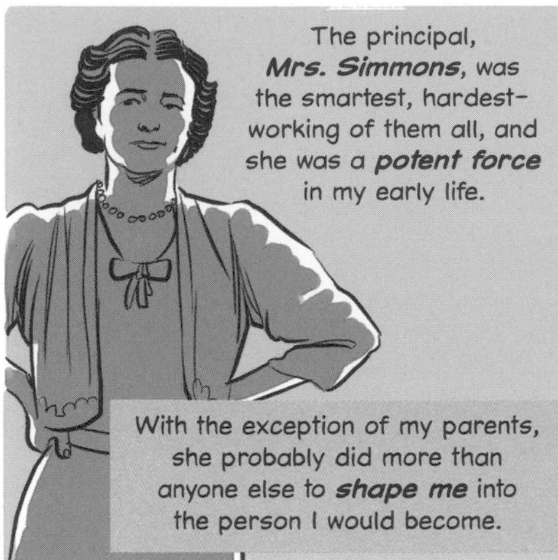
The principal, **Mrs. Simmons,** was the smartest, hardest-working of them all, and she was a **potent force** in my early life.
With the exception of my parents, she probably did more than anyone else to **shape me** into the person I would become.

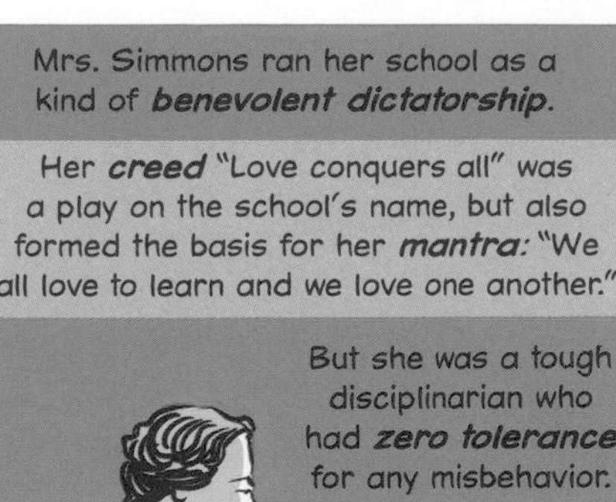
Mrs. Simmons ran her school as a kind of **benevolent dictatorship.**
Her **creed** "Love conquers all" was a play on the school's name, but also formed the basis for her **mantra:** "We all love to learn and we love one another."
But she was a tough disciplinarian who had **zero tolerance** for any misbehavior.

Mrs. Simmons would tell you in no uncertain terms of your **punishment,** and then she would call or write your parents.
"Party line" phones were often busy, so Mrs. Simmons usually **sent notes** home.

Parents would come in for a **chat.** She minced no words.
You know, there's **tough.** There's street tough—Heights tough... and then there is **prison tough.**
And trust me, friends, I can be prison tough and **beyond** if I have to be.

Mrs. Simmons and all the teachers lived in **better neighborhoods** than the Heights. Every day they would come to Love Elementary almost as if they were descending the social strata of Houston.

But more so, you could tell it in the way they **spoke,** with less of an accent.
But you never felt **condescended** to.
All the teachers had a **deep love** for not only their students and parents, but also for our **community, city, state,** and **country.**

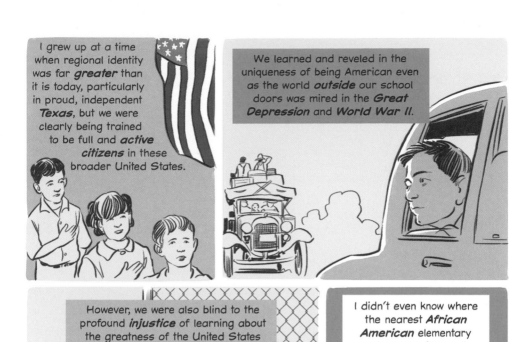

I grew up at a time when regional identity was far ***greater*** than it is today, particularly in proud, independent ***Texas***, but we were clearly being trained to be full and ***active citizens*** in these broader United States.

We learned and reveled in the uniqueness of being American even as the world ***outside*** our school doors was mired in the ***Great Depression*** and ***World War II***.

However, we were also blind to the profound ***injustice*** of learning about the greatness of the United States as students in an ***all-white school***.

I didn't even know where the nearest ***African American*** elementary school was for most of my childhood.

Despite the glaring deficit on race, my elementary school education started to give me the tools to understand my country—
ONE NATION
INDIVISIBLE
—a path that would eventually allow me to realize America's injustices as well as its strengths.

I was the first in my family ever to enter an institution of **higher learning**—
—and with our household income I was destined to attend a **public college**.
We were **college students** and the **pride** in that was palpable.
Many of my classmates were, like me, from Texas families who had **never** sent anyone to college.
A large number of the **male students** had their tuition covered by the GI Bill.
As a country, we were **determined** to knock down the doors of the middle class, rebuild our nation—
—and use education as a ladder not only for our own growth but also for **future generations**.

My college was full of dedicated educators who might not have had national reputations for the quality of their scholarship—
—but who were committed to teaching us with an idealism that today may sound a bit corny or unbelievable.
Education was a gift, part of the panoply of blessings for having the good luck to be alive at that time and in those United States.
But we didn't learn much about foreign cultures, let alone appreciate the different cultures within our own nation.
Our literary canon was almost exclusively white male authors.
Little discussion about the sins of our own history, even slavery or the plight of the Native Americans.
We didn't appreciate the full importance of science or the need to protect the environment.
Outside the classroom, we were far less sophisticated in identifying bullying and other forms of abuse.
My schools were a long way from perfect.

When I became a reporter, it didn't take long for me to see how many of the ***inequities*** in our nation were grounded in the ***limitations*** of our ***educational system.***

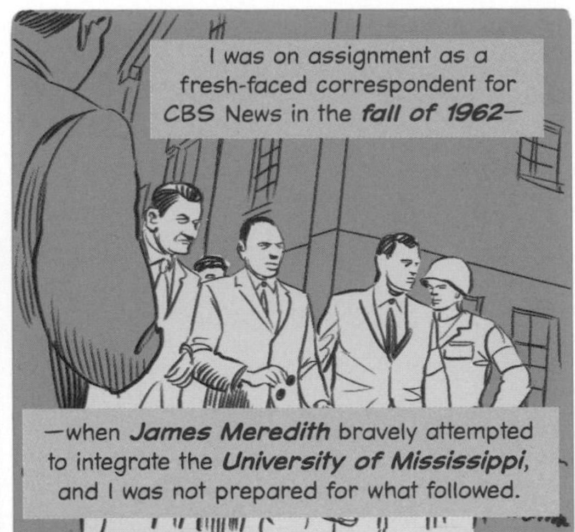
I was on assignment as a fresh-faced correspondent for CBS News in the ***fall of 1962***—
—when ***James Meredith*** bravely attempted to integrate the ***University of Mississippi***, and I was not prepared for what followed.

Just a few years removed from my own cherished college experience, I was ***deeply disturbed*** to be on a college campus, a beautiful one with a ***deep history***—
—and see the ***hate*** for a man whose crime was that he simply wanted an ***education.***

It is ***too easy*** for those who today breezily dismiss the legacy of ***race*** and ***education*** to ***forget*** what happened in places like Oxford.

We still are living in the shadow of this ***history.***

Over the years that followed, I would report on many stories that portrayed the great and ***dire inconsistencies*** in our ***public education system.***

Recently I have begun to despair, as I see the very notion of public schools under threat.

Instead of a national will to make free and open education a priority and strength, I see insidious forces—
—overtly and covertly undermining our public schools.

The crisis of our schools, especially public schools, is complex. And difficult questions abound:
Does the general school tax system need to be reevaluated?
How do we assess the impact of charter schools, and are some voucher systems worthy of consideration?
What about Wall Street's increasing involvement in for-profit schools?

What is the optimum role for teachers' unions?
TEACHERS STRIKE
795
STRIKE
The list goes on.
But there should be no dispute that if American schools don't improve, America will lose its world leadership.
And I believe that whatever system emerges in the future, it must hew to the ideals of public education:
It must be open to all, free of charge, and of the highest quality.

Instead, what we are seeing is a ***persistent*** (and in some cases increasing) ***de facto segregation*** of schools along fissures of race and economic class, between urban and suburban districts, as well as ***within cities themselves.***

We see ***rising tuitions*** at public universities—
LOAN DEPT.
—and the under-resourcing of ***community colleges***, one of the unheralded backbones of our educational community.

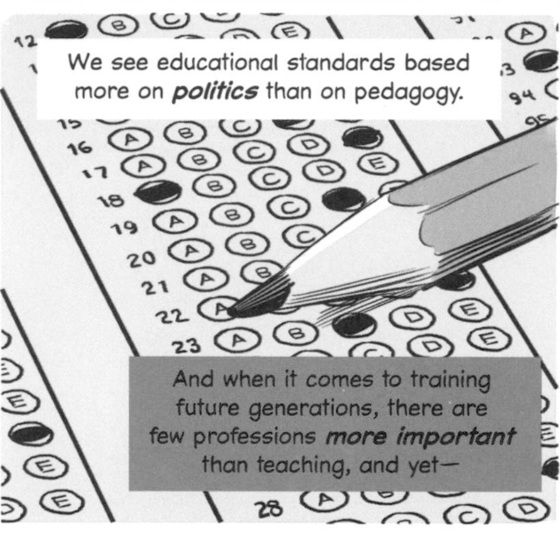
We see educational standards based more on ***politics*** than on pedagogy.
And when it comes to training future generations, there are few professions ***more important*** than teaching, and yet—

—teachers are compensated at levels out of balance with their ***responsibilities.***

During my travels to other countries, I have seen that they approach their public school systems ***differently.***
Many of the world's industrialized countries are achieving ***superior*** results.
A few years back, my reporting team and I decided to compare two ***very different*** countries whose schools are highly acclaimed.

In Finland...
Students spend less time in class, are given tremendous amounts of freedom, and have very little homework.
In Singapore...
Schools are strict and rigid; standardized tests form the basis of the educational system.
Public schools cater to everyone, almost no private schools.
It isn't just the best students who do well; every child, regardless of circumstances, has access to a good school.
Finland's students regularly score among the highest in the world.
Ninety percent of students get private tutoring to help pass exams.
The tests sort students into elite academic colleges, technical schools, or vocational training.
Singapore's students regularly score among the highest in the world.
Although Singapore and Finland are polar opposites in their educational philosophies, they have some important similarities besides just the high results for their students.
Both countries have a come a long way, fast.
Both Finland and Singapore have a rigorous commitment from their national governments to make quality schools, evenly distributed in their population, a top priority.
And there is another important key to their success. Schoolteachers are held in high esteem in both countries, and they get a lot of training and support.

Given the *current struggles* within the United States, it may be hard to remember that up until relatively *recently* our school system was the *envy* of the world.

That was an outgrowth of our *changing country*, for while some public schools existed early on—
—it was really the rise of *educational reformers* in the antebellum era that set us on the path to *true public education*.

Few loom larger than *Horace Mann*, who argued that a truly free populace could not remain *ignorant*—

—and that communities must provide *nonsectarian public schools*, staffed by trained teachers and open to students of *diverse backgrounds*.

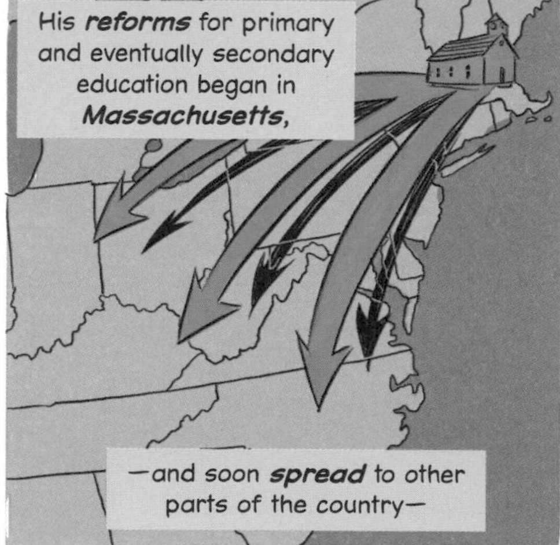
His *reforms* for primary and eventually secondary education began in *Massachusetts*,
—and soon *spread* to other parts of the country—

—especially as the nation was shifting from an *agricultural* to an *industrial* economy, and from rural areas to cities.

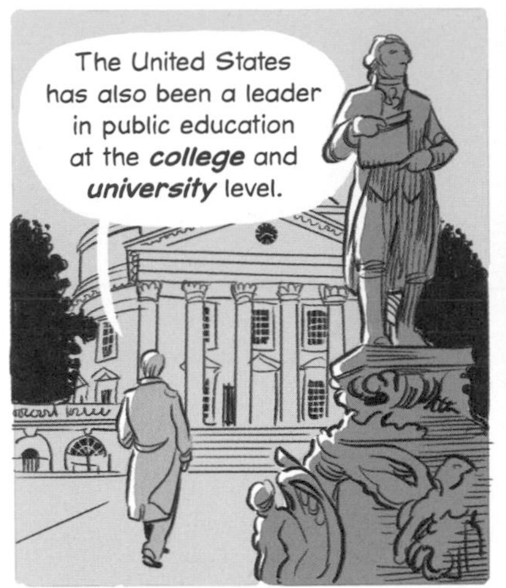
The United States has also been a leader in public education at the *college* and *university* level.

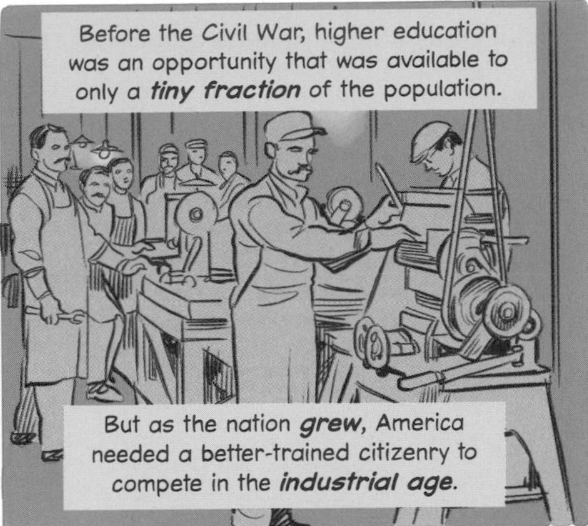
Before the Civil War, higher education was an opportunity that was available to only a *tiny fraction* of the population.
But as the nation *grew*, America needed a better-trained citizenry to compete in the *industrial age*.

So in 1862, in the midst of the *Civil War*, Congress passed and President Lincoln signed the *Morrill Act*, which set up the land *grant college system*.

These schools would be *focused* on agriculture and engineering, but they would really become *general universities*.

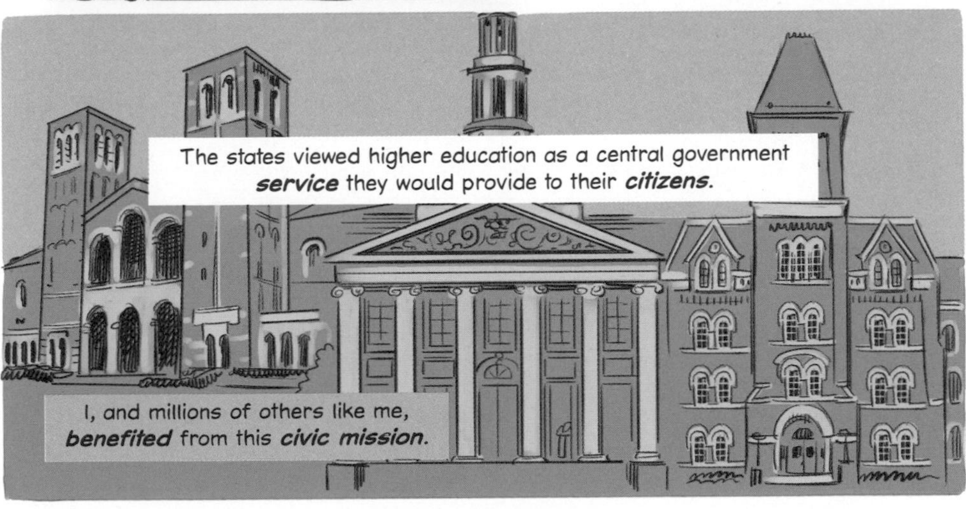
The states viewed higher education as a central government *service* they would provide to their *citizens*.
I, and millions of others like me, *benefited* from this *civic mission*.

Despite this broad **national** effort to **expand access** to education—
—**local** and **state** control of schools and state colleges has always been a **pillar** of our system.

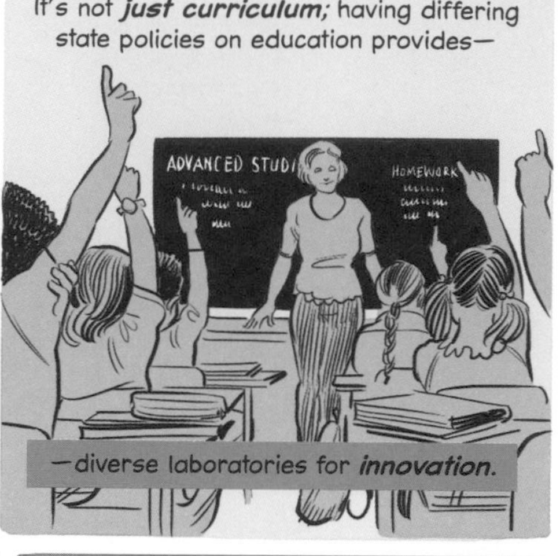
It's not **just curriculum;** having differing state policies on education provides—
HOMEWORK
—diverse laboratories for **innovation.**

But all the advantages of this decentralized system are predicated on state and local governments **believing** in the importance of **funding** high-quality education,
an instinct that is in **steep decline** in many places.
A system of local control can also distribute funding **unfairly,** as we see often today when rich suburban districts have resources that **poorer** and urban ones **do not.**

Since local control also gives communities great power to **shape curriculum,** whether it is teaching about **evolution, civil rights history,** or **climate change**—
—the **hyper-partisanship** of our nation is trickling into the classroom.

In several states, boards of education have adopted standards that **undermine the futures**—
CIVIL WAR
—of the very students these schools are **supposed** to serve.

The fight for the soul of American **public education** is one from which none of us can afford to shrink.
It is in essence a battle for the **heart, soul,** and **future** of the United States.

One of the great strengths of the public education system is that it provides a world of **second chances.**
I have seen many late bloomers **struggle** in their early years at school and later go on to a community college and transfer to a **four-year school.**

Education is not about just **planting** a **seed;** it is also about **nurturing,** over many decades—
—a productive, **meaningful,** and happy life.

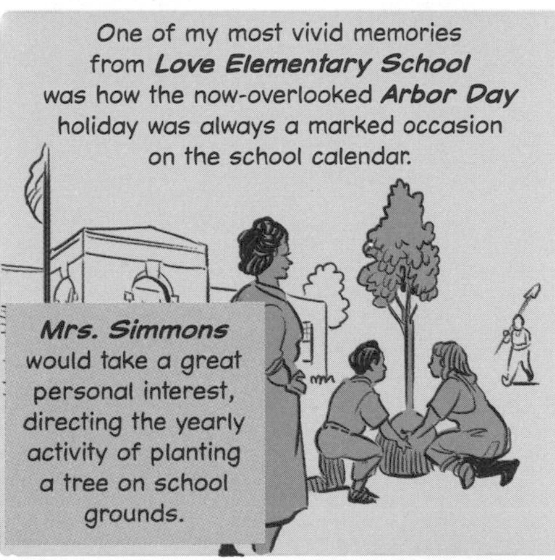
One of my most vivid memories from **Love Elementary School** was how the now-overlooked **Arbor Day** holiday was always a marked occasion on the school calendar.
Mrs. Simmons would take a great personal interest, directing the yearly activity of planting a tree on school grounds.

Each year we would gather around to see a **delicate sapling** go into the ground.
Our **responsibilities** had just begun.
In the months after the planting, we were **tasked** with nourishing the young trees into maturity.
On a recent trip to Houston with one of my grandsons, we **drove past** my old school.

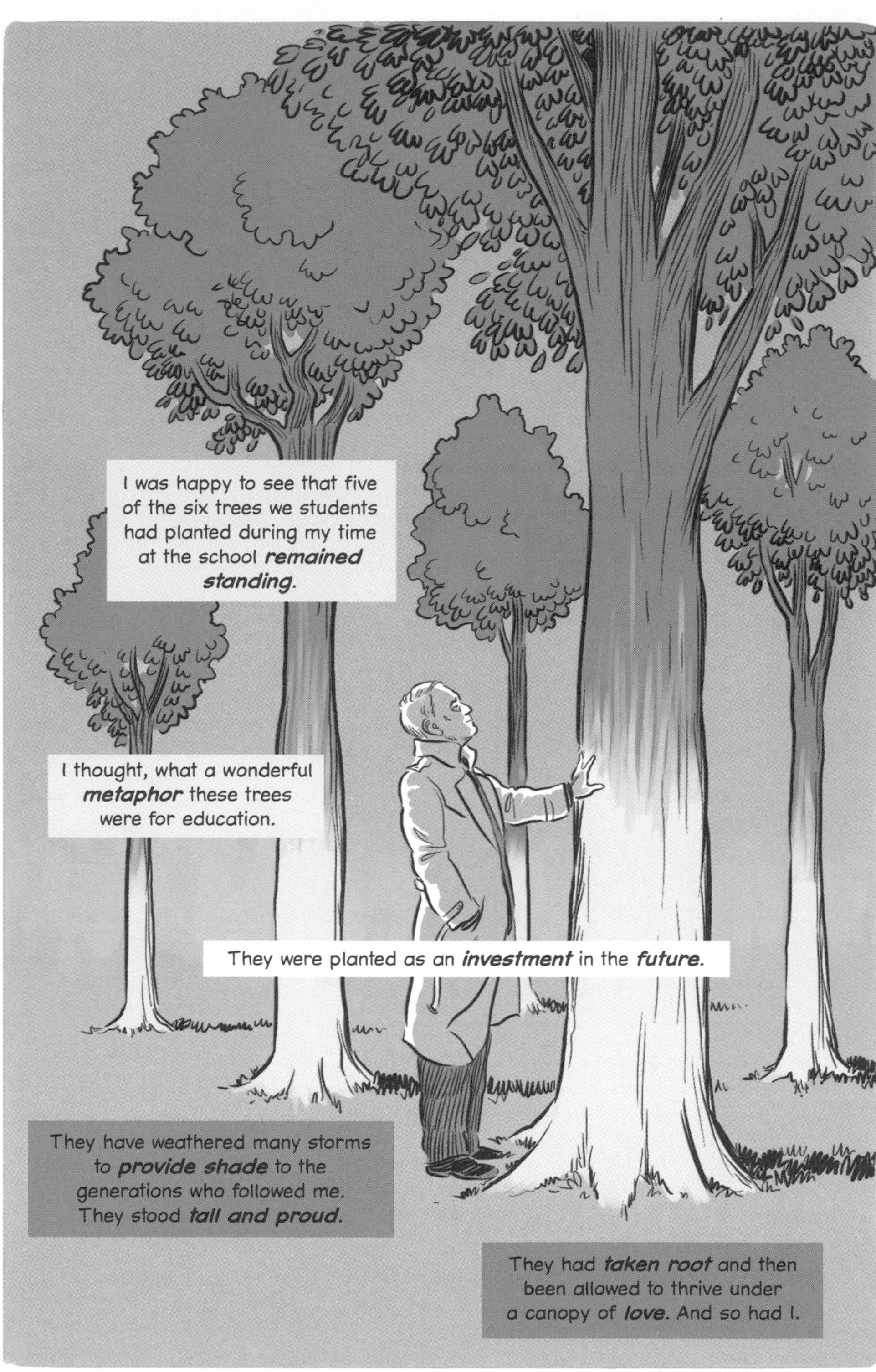
I was happy to see that five of the six trees we students had planted during my time at the school ***remained standing***.
I thought, what a wonderful ***metaphor*** these trees were for education.
They were planted as an ***investment*** in the ***future***.
They have weathered many storms to ***provide shade*** to the generations who followed me. They stood ***tall and proud***.
They had ***taken root*** and then been allowed to thrive under a canopy of ***love***. And so had I.

service

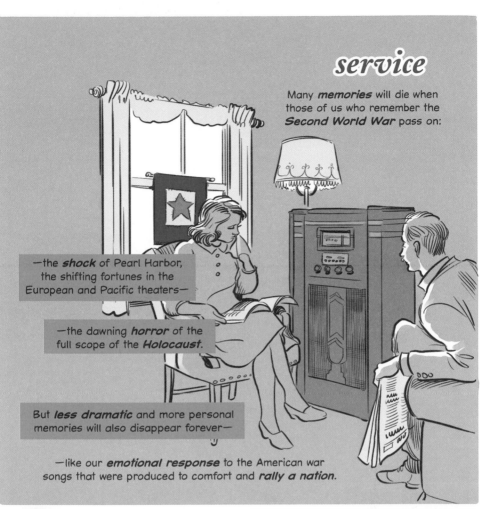

Many ***memories*** will die when those of us who remember the ***Second World War*** pass on:

—the ***shock*** of Pearl Harbor, the shifting fortunes in the European and Pacific theaters—

—the dawning ***horror*** of the full scope of the ***Holocaust***.

But ***less dramatic*** and more personal memories will also disappear forever—

—like our ***emotional response*** to the American war songs that were produced to comfort and ***rally a nation***.

To later generations, those songs of the early 1940s, with their simple tunes and lyrics that verge on (or even surpass) the jingoistic, may rise at best to the level of intellectual curiosity.

But if I hear just a few bars of many of them, my eyes sometimes dampen, and it's hard to sing the lyrics without a quiver in my voice.

The words and music *transport* me back.
The world of my youth was engulfed in a *desperate fight* for the survival of humanity, but these songs remind me that we remained in some ways *oddly innocent*.

Simple songs of heroism and sacrifice, with evocative titles like "There's a Star Spangled Banner Waving Somewhere," were welcomed and *embraced* by a grateful public without cynicism.

There is *one song* that still strikes at me harder than most, "The Ballad of Rodger Young."

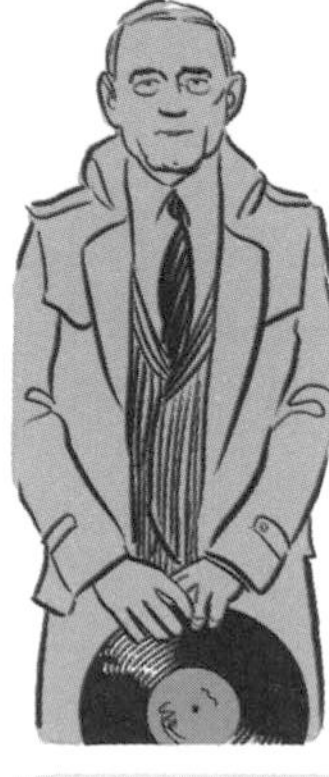

It tells the story of a young infantryman who *gave his life* so that his fellow soldiers could live.

In an *ambush* in the Solomon Islands on July 31, 1943, Young charged a Japanese pillbox.
His is a story of *uncommon valor*, but in war, I have found, such stories are not uncommon.

What shakes me to the core in this song is the *fourth stanza*, which paints a picture of Young's final resting place.

"On the island of New Georgia in the Solomons
Stands a simple wooden cross alone to tell..."

These words capture the heroism and insanity of war *writ large*.

We live in *debt* to those who have served and died, a debt *tallied* in *blood*.
And too often our *political leaders* who commit our young men, and now young women, *into war* do not take this truth into account with an adequate *fullness* of measure.
Over the years, I have been to *many* military cemeteries, and I am *always* overcome with waves of *emotion*.

For me the most *striking* hallowed ground is the *Normandy American Cemetery* in France.

9,387 American servicemen are buried here.

Death strikes us *all* with the same finality.

The cemetery is one of the most *peaceful* and *beautiful* places I have ever visited—

—a far cry from the *pain* and *torment* that led to its creation.

Most buried here lost their lives in that *fateful landing* on the nearby beaches on *D-day* or in the fierce battles that immediately followed.

You can't *help* but think:

What might they have *accomplished* if they had *lived*?

What happened to the ones they *left behind*?

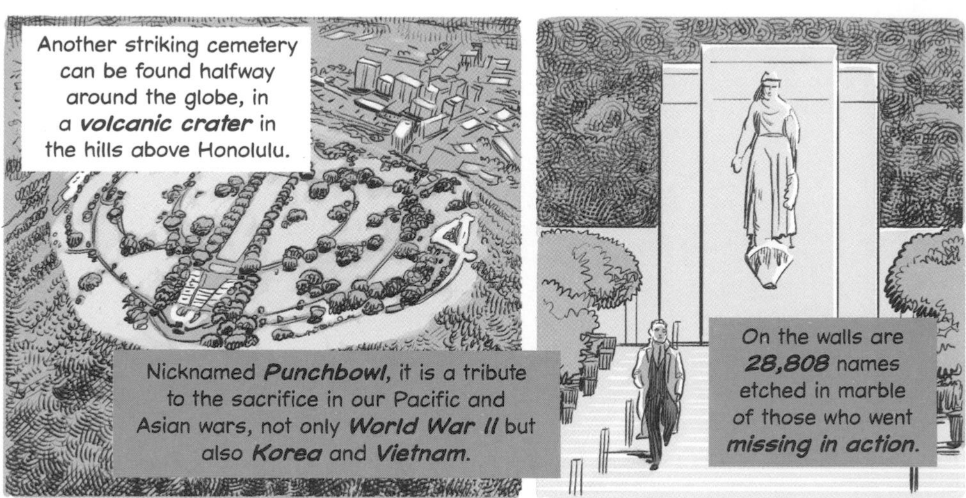
Another striking cemetery can be found halfway around the globe, in a ***volcanic crater*** in the hills above Honolulu.
Nicknamed ***Punchbowl,*** it is a tribute to the sacrifice in our Pacific and Asian wars, not only ***World War II*** but also ***Korea*** and ***Vietnam.***
On the walls are ***28,808*** names etched in marble of those who went ***missing in action.***

An inscription reads:
*"In these gardens are recorded the names of Americans who gave their lives in the service of their country and whose earthly resting place is **known only to God.**"*
War turns ***upside down*** the normal order of life—
—being ***young*** makes you more likely to ***die.***

The attack on ***Pearl Harbor*** took place on a Sunday—
—and I remember my ***father*** and his younger brother John going ***immediately*** to the recruiting office in ***downtown Houston.***
RECRUITMENT OFFICE

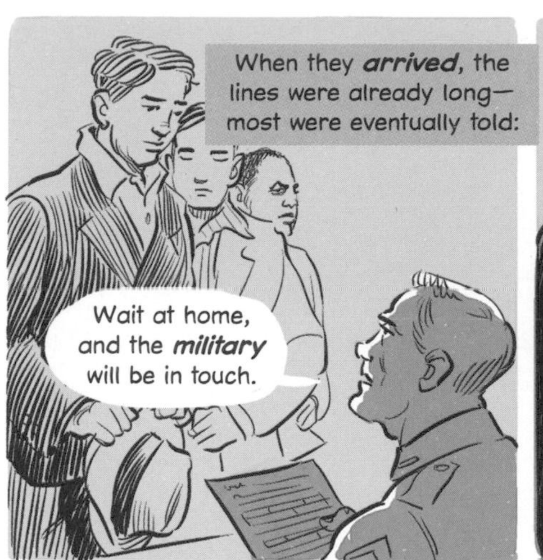
When they *arrived*, the lines were already long—most were eventually told:
Wait at home, and the *military* will be in touch.

My *father*, already in his thirties with three young children and doing what was deemed *essential* work in the oil fields, would not not end up on active military duty—
—(he later volunteered for the *civil defense units* and became our neighborhood civil watch).

My uncle John, already in his late twenties and with *flat, slightly deformed feet*, also didn't go off to war.
Their offers to volunteer for active military service were *declined*.

My uncle *Hartzell Sherrill*, who was young and single, volunteered for the Navy.
He ended up in the *merchant marines*.

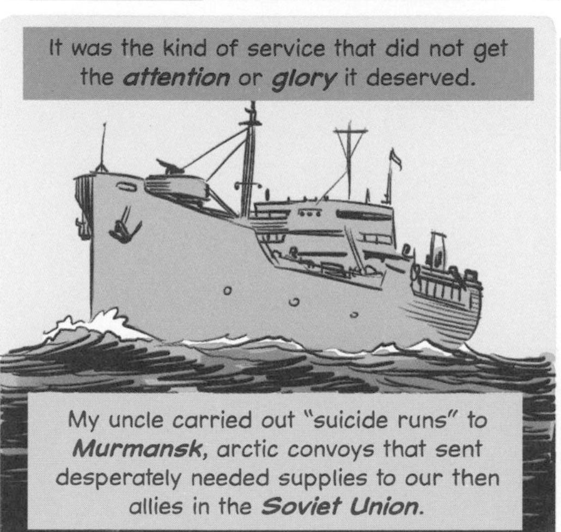
It was the kind of service that did not get the *attention* or *glory* it deserved.
My uncle carried out "suicide runs" to *Murmansk*, arctic convoys that sent desperately needed supplies to our then allies in the *Soviet Union*.

Uncle Hartzell survived, but he didn't get many *medals* for his courageous service—
—and when he returned he didn't talk about it much.
That was *common*, as well.

And that is how it was during ***World War II:***
There was a sense of ***service*** that permeated all of our society, even down to ***young boys*** like me.

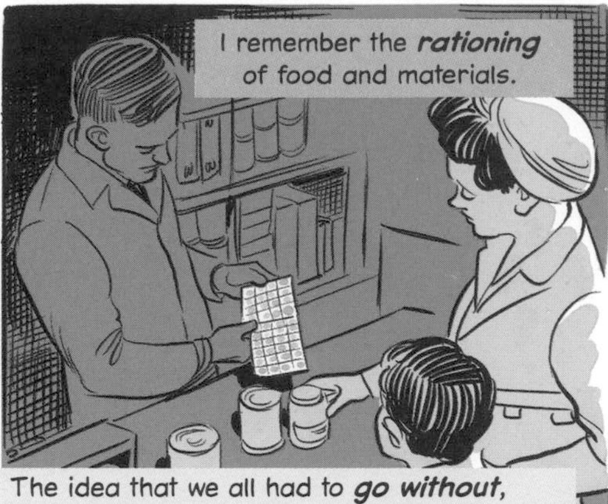
I remember the ***rationing*** of food and materials.
The idea that we all had to ***go without***, that we were all asked to sacrifice in even small ways, created a sense of ***togetherness***.

The government sponsored ***drives*** to collect spare aluminum, rubber, and the like.

SCRAP DRIVE
Looking back now, I am not sure if all this was actually ***needed*** for the war effort, or whether these drives, organized down to the neighborhood level, were meant simply to inspire a ***unity of purpose***.

Whatever the reason, my young friends and I were ***hooked***.
We would scour the creeks and bayous near our homes for ***discarded junk***.

When I collected more than any other kid in the neighborhood, I was awarded a little ribbon with what I now know to be a ***cheap metal disk***.

Bestowed, I was told, by none other than ***General Dwight D. Eisenhower*** himself.

To be decorated by the commander of Allied forces in Europe was a big source of ***pride***.

And that ***medal*** became a prized possession.

What that early experience taught me is that *service* can come in many forms.
Now we, as a nation, are in *desperate need* of expanding and celebrating the notion of *service.*

As a journalist, I often confront the *Dickensian* side of life—
—in places like prisons, county hospitals, police stations, and homeless shelters. I see *despair, desperation,* and piercing *cruelty*—

—enough to often lead me to question the *decency* of my fellow man.
But I am also struck by the many men and women I find of *deep service:* doctors, nurses, clerks, social workers, paramedics—

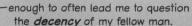

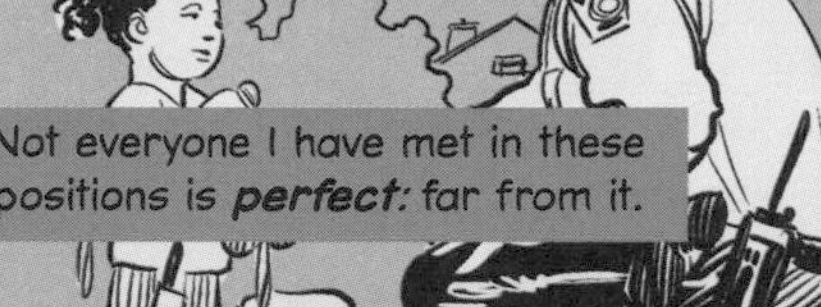
—police officers, district attorneys, public defenders, and so on.
Not everyone I have met in these positions is *perfect:* far from it.
But the *vast majority* are committed to their work and to making difficult and painful situations less difficult and painful.

And then there are those I've met in my travels around the United States who give of themselves *every day* to strengthen their communities.
They are teachers, firefighters, and guidance counselors. They volunteer in nursing homes and youth centers.

They are part of an America of largely *unapplauded service,* but most who do this work have no interest in seeking recognition.

They understand that each act of assistance is a vote of confidence in our *common humanity.*

I am **proud** that both of my children went into careers of **public service**, giving up more lucrative paths to help their communities—

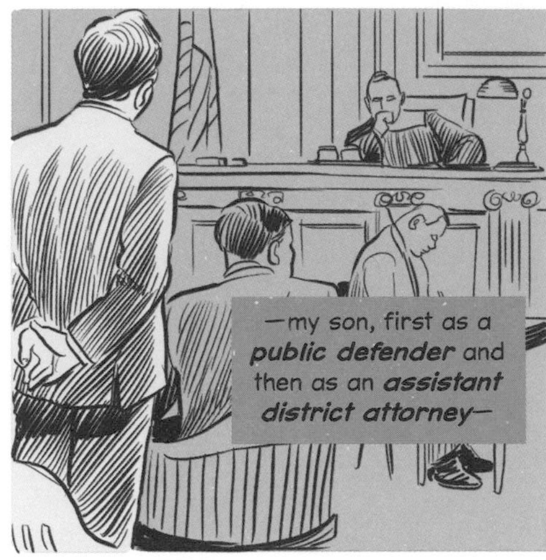
—my son, first as a **public defender** and then as an **assistant district attorney**—

—and my daughter as a leader in **environmental and civic causes.**

My wife, **Jean**, has provided an example, **volunteering** for years—
—and bringing children with learning disabilities and from **underprivileged homes** into our own home to teach them how to **read.**

None of my family members will tell you that they should be **recognized** for their actions.
They understand that they are blessed with much and that others **do far more.**
They see all this as their **duty** to country.
This is how widespread and **common** service really is.

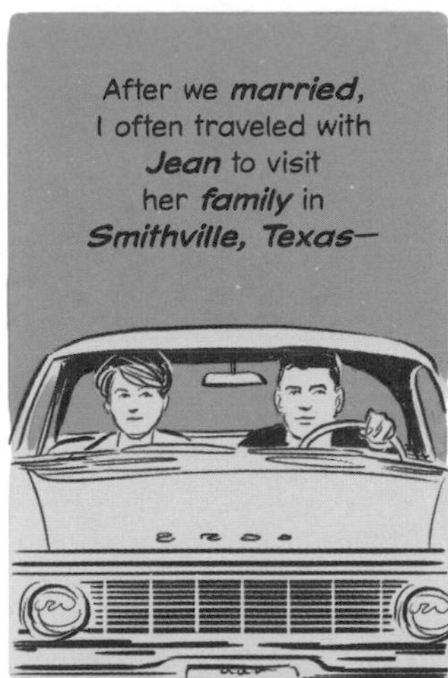
After we **married**, I often traveled with **Jean** to visit her **family** in **Smithville, Texas**—

—and one **favorite** activity was sitting in on the town's **council meetings**, on which my father-in-law served.
This was bottom-up democracy, infused with **real public service.**

Perhaps it is not controversial to write glowingly of a small-town democracy that resembled a scene from a **Norman Rockwell** painting—

—but that same sense of **purpose** and **service** fills our great capital city.
"Washington" has become for many a **dirty word** that connotes self-serving politicians and **devious** lobbyists. To be sure, **they are there**, but when I first arrived—

—I was struck by how populated the government was with **young people** from every corner of the nation, there to do the **right thing** and serve their country.
Yes, you see ambition, but also **idealism** and the desire to work hard. You see **purpose** and **patriotism**. It is bipartisan.

This is a part of Washington that doesn't get **nearly** enough attention.

Many who work in the government agencies could earn a ***better salary*** for less work in the ***private sector***, yet they work here because they believe in ***service to country***.
Can government bureaucracies be infuriating and inefficient? ***Of course***.

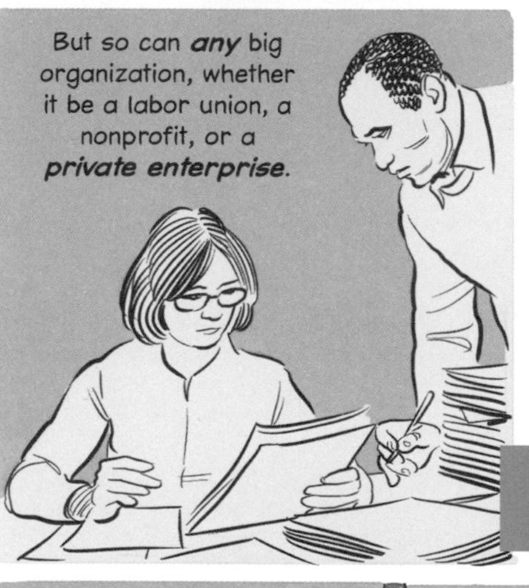
But so can ***any*** big organization, whether it be a labor union, a nonprofit, or a ***private enterprise***.

To be sure, there are problems with Washington, but most of them can be found on ***Capitol Hill*** and K Street and in the White House, not in the windowless offices of the Environmental Protection Agency or the State Department.
And then there are all the Americans serving ***around the globe***, representing our nation in official and unofficial capacities.

There is our ***diplomatic corps***, not only the political ambassadors, but often more impressively the ***career workers***—the quiet Americans—who toil in difficult and sometimes dangerous locales with little to ***no recognition*** for their service.

There are ***Peace Corps volunteers*** and leaders of nongovernmental organizations who build schools, treat disease, and deliver clean water.
Service to our country is about not only helping us and ours, but also ***taking care of others*** around the world.

In 2004, just after most of us had gone to bed on *Christmas*—

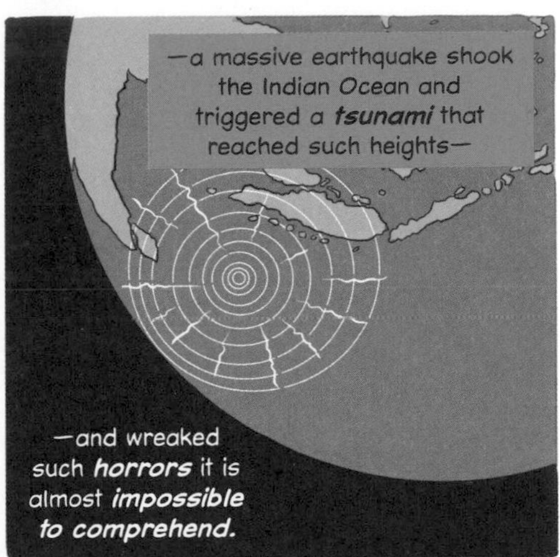
—a massive earthquake shook the Indian Ocean and triggered a *tsunami* that reached such heights—
—and wreaked such *horrors* it is almost *impossible to comprehend.*

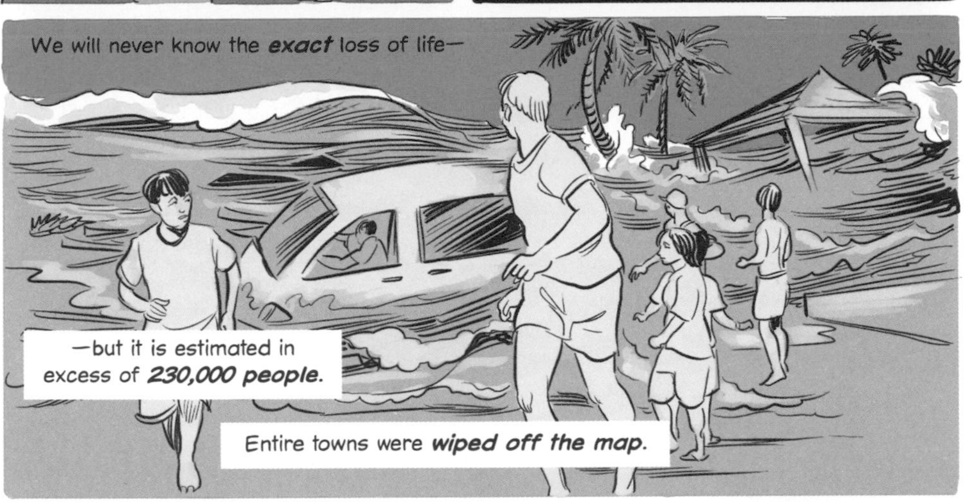
We will never know the *exact* loss of life—
—but it is estimated in excess of *230,000 people*.
Entire towns were *wiped off the map*.

CBS NEWS
The rest of the world, *preoccupied* with end-of-year celebrations, was *slow* to react.
Even at CBS News, I had to *convince* the president of the news division that this was *worthy* of intensive coverage.

On December 31, I was on a plane for *60 Minutes,* along with my producers **Chris Martin** and **Elliot Kirschner**.

The United States military had dispatched the aircraft carrier USS *Abraham Lincoln* to the waters off the coast of the Indonesian island of **Sumatra**.

The next morning we took off for the **disaster zone**. Out of my window I could see beautifully vegetated coastlines of steep cliffs—
—but the trees and plants didn't reach the sea. Instead there was a **tall band of brown dirt**.
The wall of water, perhaps as high as **eighty to a hundred feet**, had struck with such force that it ripped away everything in its path.

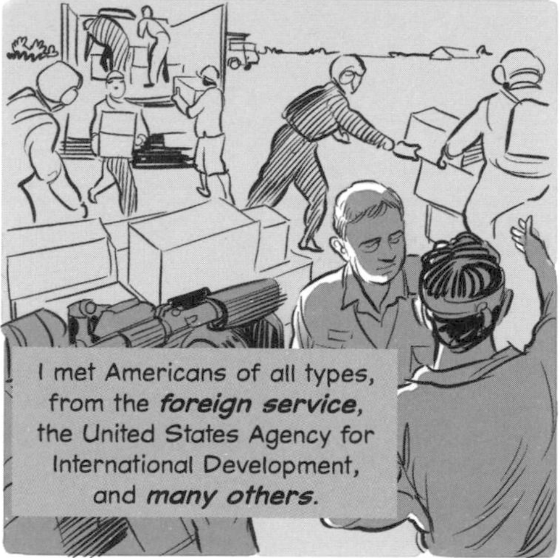
I met Americans of all types, from the **foreign service**, the United States Agency for International Development, and **many others**.

We took off with supplies for nearby **Banda Aceh**, where tens of thousands had lost their lives.

After waiting for aid for days, the first outsiders they saw were ***young Americans*** handing out food and medicine.

It was one of the most ***difficult*** stories I have ever covered—
but my spirits were ***soothed slightly*** by witnessing this level of dedicated ***service*** from my countrymen and -women.

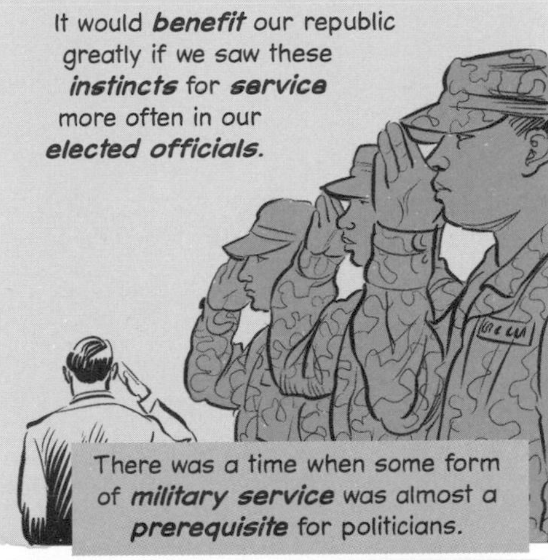
It would ***benefit*** our republic greatly if we saw these ***instincts*** for ***service*** more often in our ***elected officials***.
There was a time when some form of ***military service*** was almost a ***prerequisite*** for politicians.

While I have ***great respect*** for the military, I do not think that should be the only service ***recognized***.
Seth Moulton is a product of a fancy boarding school who has a degree in physics from ***Harvard***.
But he completed four tours in ***Iraq*** as a ***marine officer*** in combat when he could have had a far easier and more ***comfortable*** life.

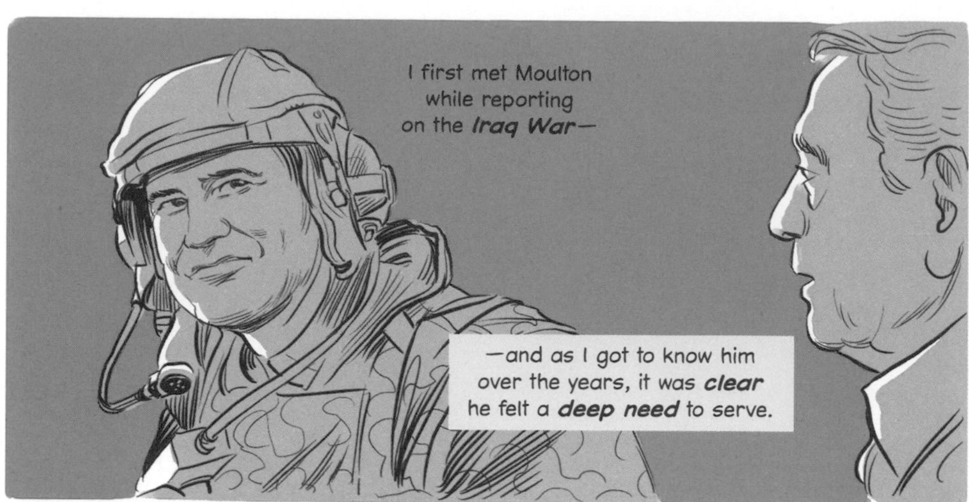
I first met Moulton while reporting on the ***Iraq War***—
—and as I got to know him over the years, it was ***clear*** he felt a ***deep need*** to serve.

While running for office, it was revealed that he had received numerous ***combat medals*** in Iraq for his service—
—and he hadn't even told his ***parents***.

There is a healthy ***disrespect*** among ***veterans*** who served on the front lines for people who walk around telling ***war stories***.
There were many ***others*** who did heroic things and received ***no awards*** at all.

That is the benefit of service: it tends to ***humanize*** you.
It's about the ***values*** that drive a person to ***help*** by joining a mission that is ***bigger*** than they are.
When politicians from their ***gilded perch*** in Washington cut funding for foreign aid programs, I am ***troubled***.

When they ***denigrate*** government workers, I am ***indignant***.
And when they send the men and women who ***volunteered*** for our armed forces to multiple tours of combat while asking ***nothing*** of sacrifice from the rest of us, I am ***angry***.

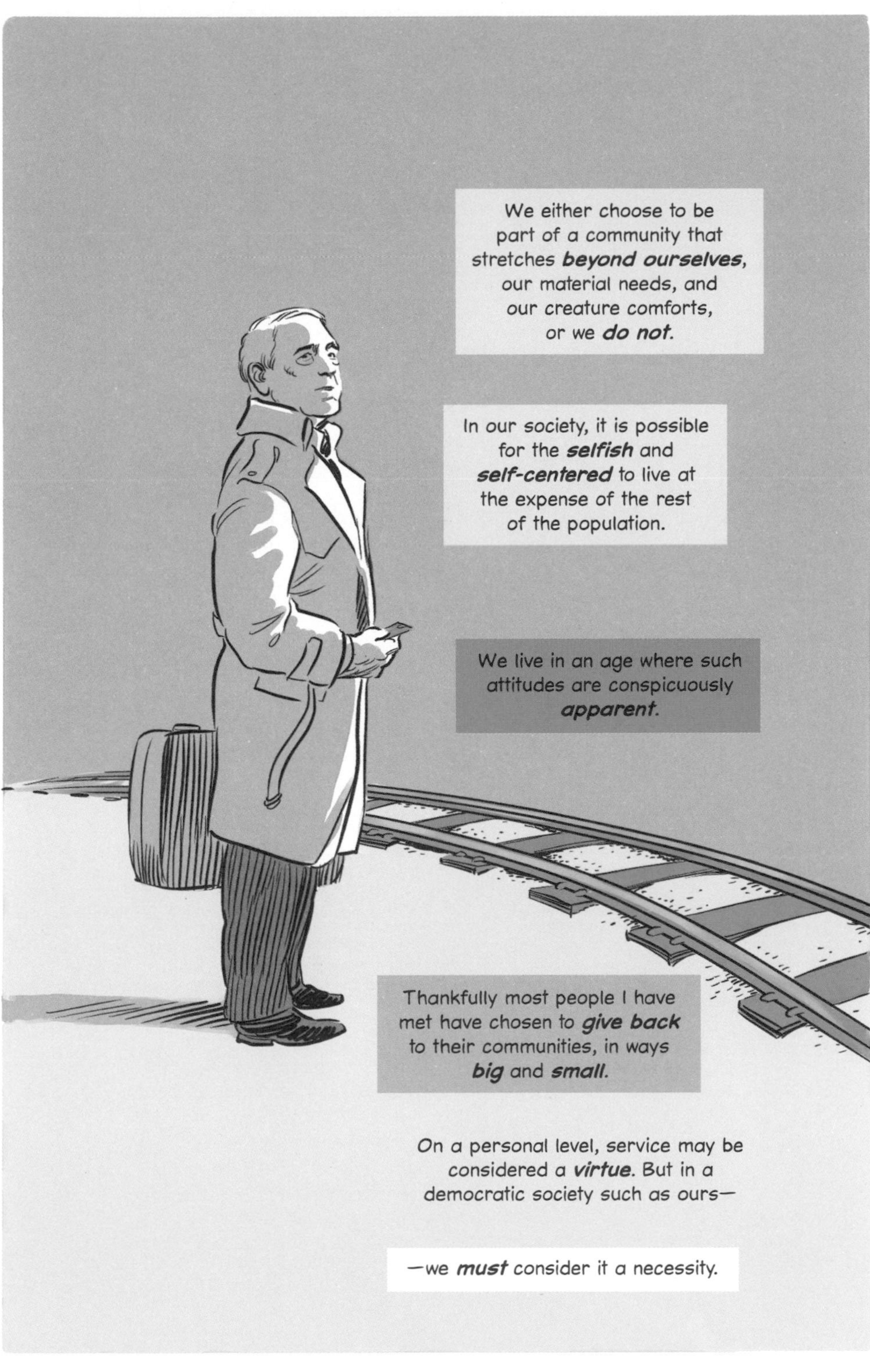
We either choose to be part of a community that stretches ***beyond ourselves***, our material needs, and our creature comforts, or we ***do not***.
In our society, it is possible for the ***selfish*** and ***self-centered*** to live at the expense of the rest of the population.
We live in an age where such attitudes are conspicuously ***apparent***.
Thankfully most people I have met have chosen to ***give back*** to their communities, in ways ***big*** and ***small***.
On a personal level, service may be considered a ***virtue***. But in a democratic society such as ours—
—we ***must*** consider it a necessity.

6

character

audacity

It was ***Abraham Lincoln*** who authorized the first ***transcontinental railroad*** during the Civil War.

How ***audacious.***

By the time I was born, architecturally stunning ***train stations*** bustled at the heart of almost every American city—

—and as a child I would ***marvel*** at the mighty locomotives pulling the ***nation forward*** in their billowing wake.

I'm old enough to remember with fondness the original ***Penn Station*** in New York City, which was modeled on one of the great ruins of ***Rome.***

While those ruins remain today, the old Penn Station does not—having been demolished in the 1960s, ostensibly in the ***service of progress.***

I still love taking the train, but I now have to leave New York through the new *Penn Station*—
PENN STATION
—one of the most *dispiriting* buildings in America.

It's a warren of *dirty* underground hallways, and it embodies the *opposite* of audacity: it is *utilitarian*, *cost-beneficial*, and utterly *uninspired*.

Yale architecture professor *Vincent Scully Jr.* lamented, "One entered the city like a god; one scuttles in now like a rat."

While I like to ride *Amtrak's* high-speed *Acela* line, it is also a bit disappointing—a *reminder* that the United States long ago *lost* its lead on rail to the great trains of Europe and Asia.

Work often takes me to Washington, D.C., and as I pull into the beautifully renovated *Union Station*, I begin to feel better.
I emerge to see the *mighty Capitol dome*, and I wonder:

If we were building the Capitol today, would we make it so *bold* and *beautiful*?
American greatness has largely been driven by *audacity*.

Thirteen far-flung colonies challenged, and defeated, the mighty *British army*.
A Constitution written more than *two centuries ago* has outlined a stable form of government.

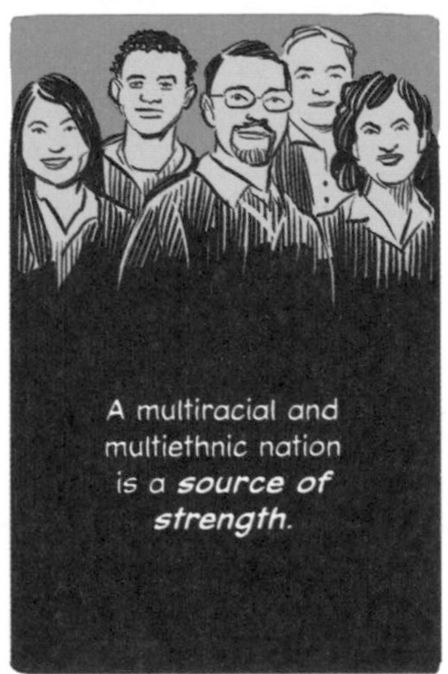
A multiracial and multiethnic nation is a *source of strength*.

A free and open society has allowed us to push the boundaries of *human knowledge* and *exploration*.

I often think about this national proclivity toward boldness when I step out on the porch of my favorite fishing cabin and look to the sparkling night sky.

Seeing all those stars and a brilliant moon, I reflect on how, during my childhood, the idea of travel into the heavens existed only in the imagination of fiction writers such as Jules Verne.

But then we sent a man to the moon—

—launched robotic explorations of Mars—

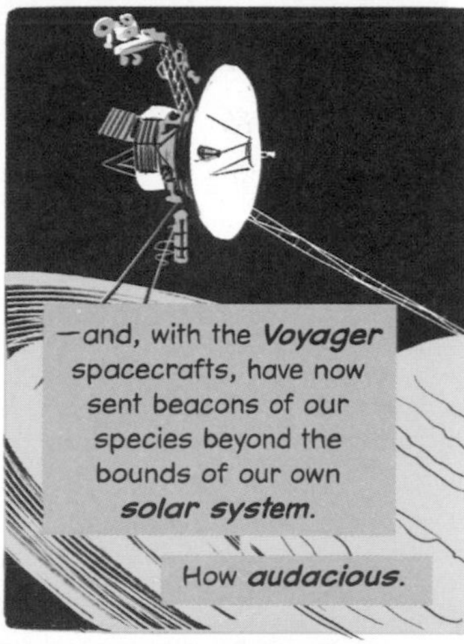
—and, with the Voyager spacecrafts, have now sent beacons of our species beyond the bounds of our own solar system.
How audacious.

Today, the space dreamers that capture public attention are private-sector mavericks like Elon Musk and Richard Branson—
—whose goals keep us relatively close to Earth.
Although NASA still boasts brilliant scientists and determined public servants, it increasingly has faded from public view into just another quiet governmental bureaucracy.
NASA
Somehow the desire for bold exploration has ebbed among our elected officials.

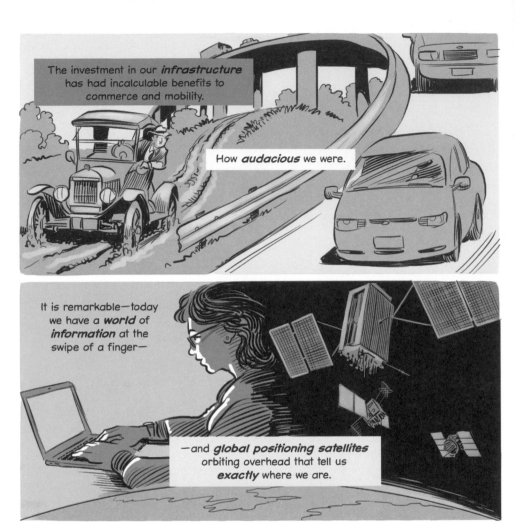

The investment in our ***infrastructure*** has had incalculable benefits to commerce and mobility.

How ***audacious*** we were.

It is remarkable—today we have a ***world*** of ***information*** at the swipe of a finger—

—and ***global positioning satellites*** orbiting overhead that tell us ***exactly*** where we are.

In a few short decades, this audacious spirit has transformed all aspects of modern life—
—even if we now take it for granted.

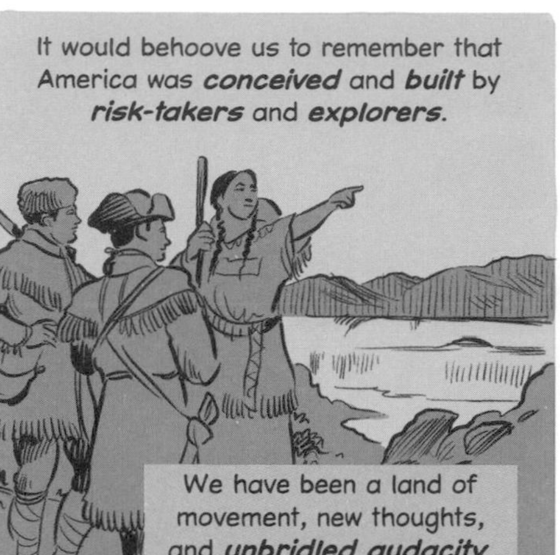
It would behoove us to remember that America was ***conceived*** and ***built*** by ***risk-takers*** and ***explorers.***
We have been a land of movement, new thoughts, and ***unbridled audacity.***

One of the hallmarks of our national character is that we have, in the past at least, been quick to ***adapt to change.***
We have even ***thrived*** in eras of ***great transformation.***

For most of my lifetime, this has been a ***two-way conversation*** between ***government*** and ***society at large.***
We expected ourselves and those we elected to office to ***dream big*** and experiment, without fear of the failures that are invariably part of tackling ***tough challenges.***

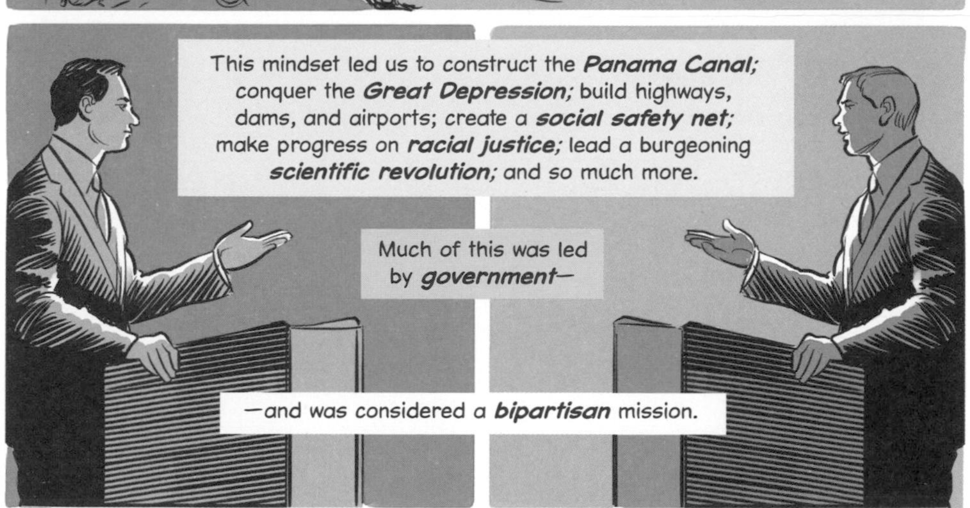
This mindset led us to construct the ***Panama Canal;*** conquer the ***Great Depression;*** build highways, dams, and airports; create a ***social safety net;*** make progress on ***racial justice;*** lead a burgeoning ***scientific revolution;*** and so much more.
Much of this was led by ***government***—
—and was considered a ***bipartisan*** mission.

It is true that **big actions** can also have big unintended **consequences.**
The **transcontinental railroad** opened up the frontier—
—but it also sped the **subjugation** of the Native Americans and the **exploitation** of Chinese immigrant labor.
Our **highway system** helped spur the primacy of the automobile—
—with its attending **urban sprawl** and **pollution.**
The era of **dam building** provided water for us to drink and grow our crops, generated electricity, and protected against floods—
—but we now know that many dams also had **severe** environmental consequences.
We cannot be **afraid** to act big, but we also cannot be afraid to **reassess** and address **problems** that may arise.
When did we begin to accept a **can't-do spirit** from so many of our national leaders?
I'm not sure when this **erosion** began.
If you had told me that I would outlive the **first great era** of **human space exploration,** I never would have believed it.

When President John F. Kennedy came to Houston in September 1962 to issue a call to explore space,
I was a young reporter excited to cover a big national story.
SEAL OF THE PRESIDENT OF THE UNITED STATES
I remember thinking that the real unknown was whether we could do it.

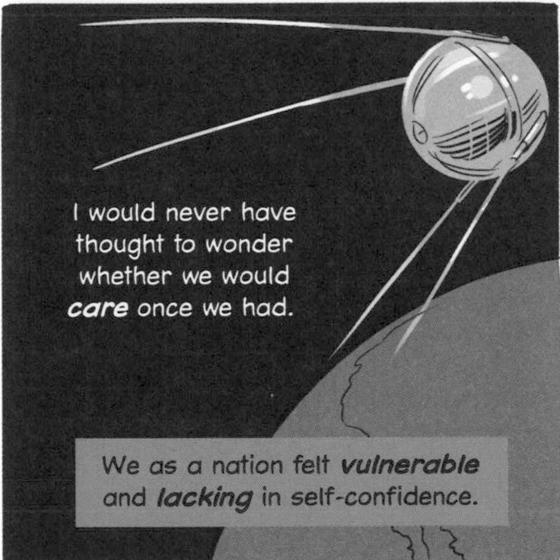
I would never have thought to wonder whether we would care once we had.
We as a nation felt vulnerable and lacking in self-confidence.

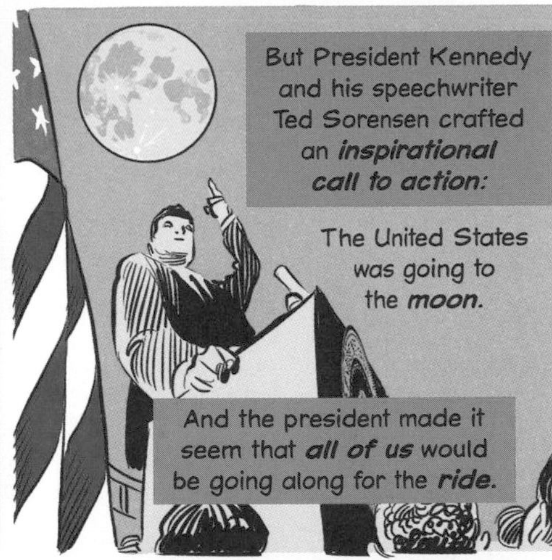
But President Kennedy and his speechwriter Ted Sorensen crafted an inspirational call to action:
The United States was going to the moon.
And the president made it seem that all of us would be going along for the ride.

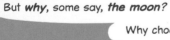

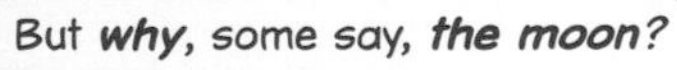
But why, some say, the moon?

Why choose this as our goal?
We choose to go to the moon in this decade and do the other things, not because they are easy, but because they are hard—
because that goal will serve to organize and measure the best of our energies and skills—
because that challenge is one that we are willing to accept, one we are unwilling to postpone, and one which we intend to win.

The president called it a choice, but it felt like a patriotic duty, full of optimism with a dash of dread at the thought that we might fail.

For those of you who were not yet born, who did not live through it, this moment must now seem pregnant with portent in ways we could never have imagined.
Who knew that this vibrant young president would be slain a little more than a year later?

Who could have imagined that after a handful of landings on the moon—
—no human from any country would thus far get close to doing it again?

Trying to summon that day in Houston, I keep returning to an image:
the grass at Rice Stadium, the site of the speech, was damp.
I was about to hear a speech calling for human beings to slip the bonds of Earth, and a shiver of remembrance shot through me.

Five years earlier, I had also been standing on ***wet grass*** pondering the heavens.

Sputnik, the first man-made satellite, had been launched by the ***Soviets*** in ***1957***.

It was a ***shock*** to our national confidence that would culminate in ***Kennedy's speech*** and the ***race*** to the ***moon***. But while Sputnik ***scared*** American policymakers, it ***awed me*** and many of my fellow countrymen.

I looked up and there it was.

I was about ***four years old*** and in the yard at my grandmother's house:

Put your ***hands*** in the dirt, Danny,

Feel the richness of the dirt and then look to the ***stars***.

Standing there at ***Rice Stadium***, remembering ***Sputnik***, I also thought of a far more distant moment, the ***first memory*** I have of my life.

I was of this land, was the message from Grandma Paige. And yet I believe I ***sensed***, even then, that there would be other ***horizons to ponder***.

Audacity is not without ***risk***, and exploration has always been about ***uncertainty*** as well as knowledge.

It's about forging forward in the face of ***likely disappointment***, even ***death***. Kennedy knew this.

As we set sail we ask God's blessing on the most ***hazardous*** and ***dangerous*** and ***greatest adventure*** on which man has ever embarked.

When we did land on the moon by the end of the 1960s, there was a sense that we were just beginning.
I, into my fourth decade of life, hoped to travel into the great void—perhaps to be the first journalist in space.

That, of course, *didn't happen*. And more broadly—and importantly—most of the predictions for piloted spaceflight *never* came true.

The timeline for a trip to *Mars* still stretches onward with its own uncertain horizon.
Our national *will* has changed.

We seem to find money for *tax cuts* for the wealthy and *foreign wars*—
—but not enough for the *exploration of space*.

In the decades *since* the moon landing—
—the biggest stories around human spaceflight have been the *tragedies*, not the triumphs.

In 1986 came the *shock* and catastrophe of the *Challenger* space shuttle explosion, which killed all seven crew members aboard, including schoolteacher *Christa McAuliffe*.
NASA
CHRISTA

As I sat at the anchor desk that day covering the *breaking news*—
—struggling, along with a *shocked nation*, to understand what had *happened*,

I remember showing viewers the *haunting pictures* of the high school students in *Concord, New Hampshire*—
—who had gathered to see their *teacher* go into *space*.
The memory *still* moves me.

That night, President Ronald Reagan addressed the nation:
I know it is hard to understand, but sometimes painful things like this happen.
It's all part of the process of exploration and discovery.
It's all part of taking a chance and expanding man's horizons.
The future doesn't belong to the fainthearted; it belongs to the brave. The Challenger crew was pulling us into the future, and we'll continue to follow them.
President Reagan promised to continue the "quest in space," and indeed, after a moratorium, the space shuttle program was renewed—
—but another tragedy would hit with the explosion of the Columbia space shuttle in 2003 and the deaths of seven more astronauts.
Even some scientists think that sending people into space isn't worth the cost and risk.
President Kennedy understood that there is something in the human character that can rally to big causes.
A nation is strengthened when it can focus on a purpose.
This impulse can be harnessed to ill effects, like wars of conquest.
Or it can be used to turn unlikely dreams into reality.

At the same time the United States was closing in on the moon—
—the country embarked on a mission back on Earth that couldn't have been more different in spirit or objective.

Whereas the space race was one of sharp national competition, this other effort would be deeply collaborative.

The goal was to eradicate the deadliest killer known to man: smallpox.

Like our voyages to the moon, this unprecedented public health mission was grounded in the audacious belief—
—that our government could do something seemingly impossible, something that would change the course of human history.

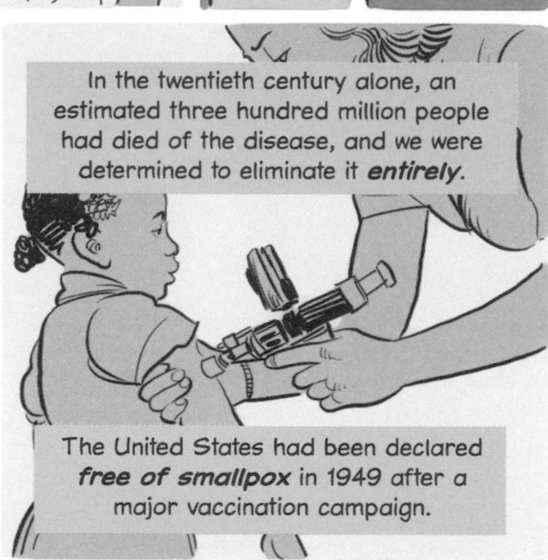
In the twentieth century alone, an estimated three hundred million people had died of the disease, and we were determined to eliminate it entirely.
The United States had been declared free of smallpox in 1949 after a major vaccination campaign.

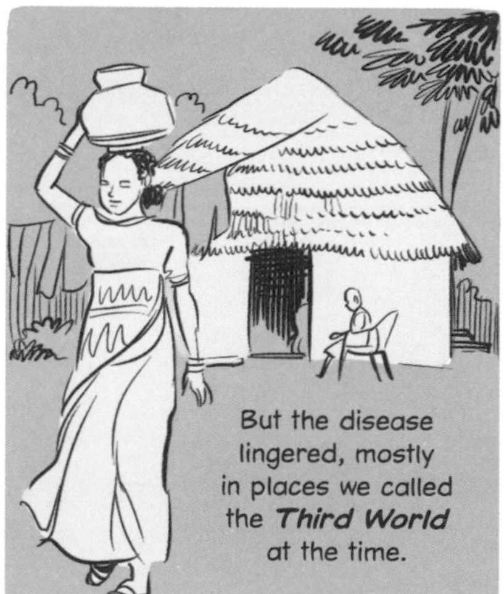
But the disease lingered, mostly in places we called the Third World at the time.

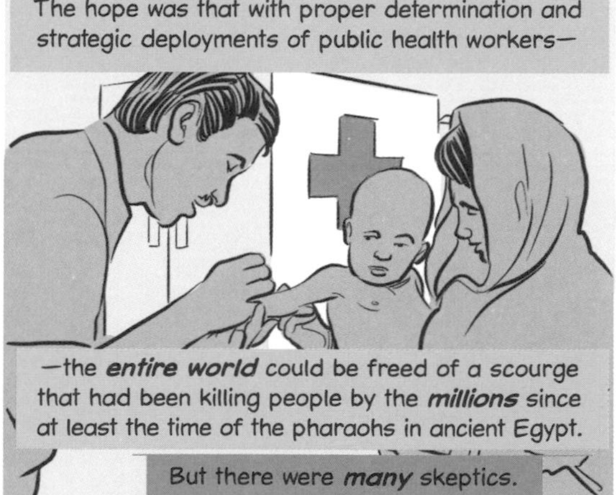
The hope was that with proper determination and strategic deployments of public health workers—
—the entire world could be freed of a scourge that had been killing people by the millions since at least the time of the pharaohs in ancient Egypt.
But there were many skeptics.

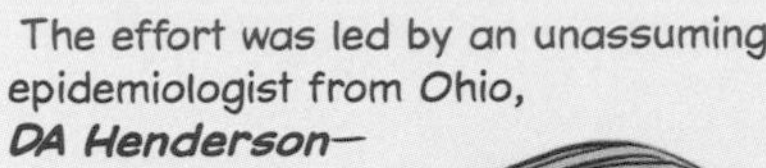

The effort was led by an unassuming epidemiologist from Ohio, ***DA Henderson***—

—(born just 150 or so miles away from fellow Buckeye, ***Neil Armstrong***).

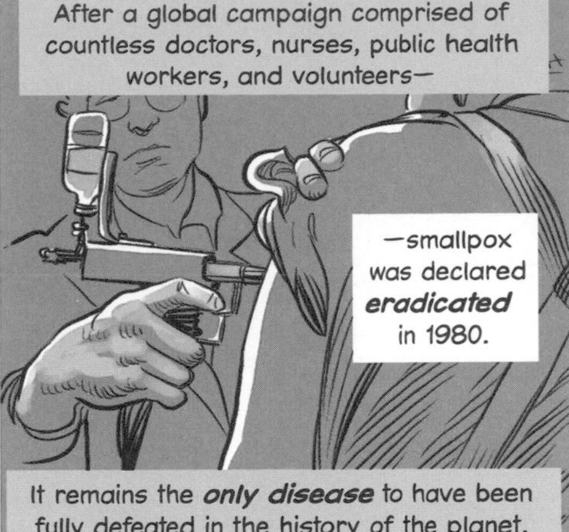

After a global campaign comprised of countless doctors, nurses, public health workers, and volunteers—
—smallpox was declared ***eradicated*** in 1980.
It remains the ***only disease*** to have been fully defeated in the history of the planet.

The eradication of smallpox has been called the ***greatest medical event*** in human history.

But the science behind it was relatively ***simple*** and well known.

There had actually been a form of ***smallpox vaccine*** since the eighteenth century.

What was required was the ability to ***dream big***, to work with others, and to see the destiny of the United States—

—as improving the lives of those ***beyond our borders***.

We see ***such ingenuity*** in America.
UAW
We do not need a heavy hand, just ***wise policies*** and a understanding that some things are ***so big or risky*** that only the government can be the ***catalyst for action***.

One of the ***greatest challenges*** of our time is the need to generate ***abundant*** and ***nonpolluting energy***.
Early dreamers learned how to harness the ***wind*** to power their ***ships;*** later we learned the power of ***steam,*** and then ***fossil fuels***.

But today we see the ***dangers*** of our ***warming planet***.
Bold leadership could rally the nation to a ***revolution*** in ***clean energy***.

It should be clear to our political leaders that a ***new energy strategy*** could be the next ***technological revolution*** America could ***lead***.
Our planet and our ***national prosperity*** are already ***suffering*** from the decline in our leadership.

At a time when we desperately need to *think boldly* about the challenges before us—
—we find many of our politicians arguing that we need to be *less ambitious.*
We hear from *too many* in Congress about why action is *difficult,* why something *cannot be done.*
Many of our government agencies were turned over to people who are actively seeking to *undermine* the mission of those agencies.
And our national needs go *unaddressed.*
It is impossible to try and *freeze* ourselves in the status quo—
—and even more impossible to return to some *mythic* and *misremembered* glorious past.

We need to remain a nation of ***new ideas*** and ***new initiatives***—
—or we will cease to be the ***strong*** and ***daring country*** I know and ***love.***

steady

It was a winter night in ***late 1973,*** and as was ***common*** during those days, I was coming home well after my children had ***gone to bed.***

My wife, ***Jean,*** was waiting for me at the small kitchen table in our town house in the Georgetown neighborhood of ***Washington, D.C.***

Are we going to be ***okay***?

It was a fair and honest question, and one for which I could not offer any of the ***assurances*** that I wished I had.

She had heard the concern from neighbors and friends—

—***whisperings*** that CBS News and, in particular, I, as the chief White House correspondent, were out on a limb on this ***Watergate story***.

We have ***everything*** on the table—

—there's no place for us to run.

Either ***history*** is going to prove us right, or I will be ***looking*** for a new line of work.

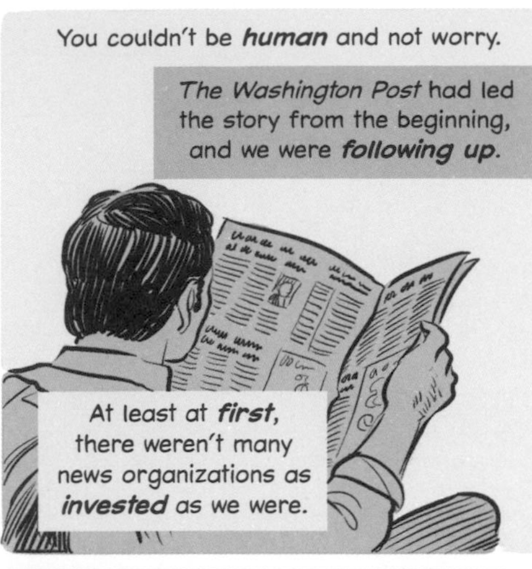
You couldn't be **human** and not worry.
The Washington Post had led the story from the beginning, and we were **following up**.
At least at **first**, there weren't many news organizations as **invested** as we were.

I worried that the *New York Times*, which had excellent reporters, was being **circumspect**.
What did **they** know that I **didn't?**

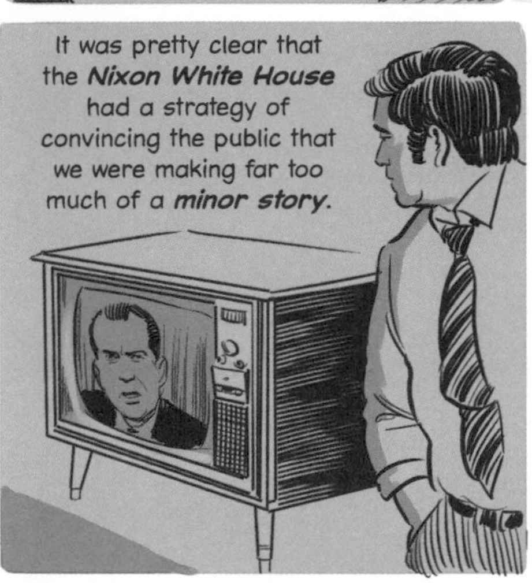
It was pretty clear that the **Nixon White House** had a strategy of convincing the public that we were making far too much of a **minor story**.

They tried to **destabilize** us.
But in the end, they **failed**, as they would eventually fail with the country at large.

At first, most of America wasn't paying very much **attention** to Watergate, but as developments began to tumble forth, the public became **transfixed**.

I think most people were not surprised that our checks and balances remained **resilient**.
I felt a **supreme belief** among the citizenry that we were a nation of **laws** and not of **men**.

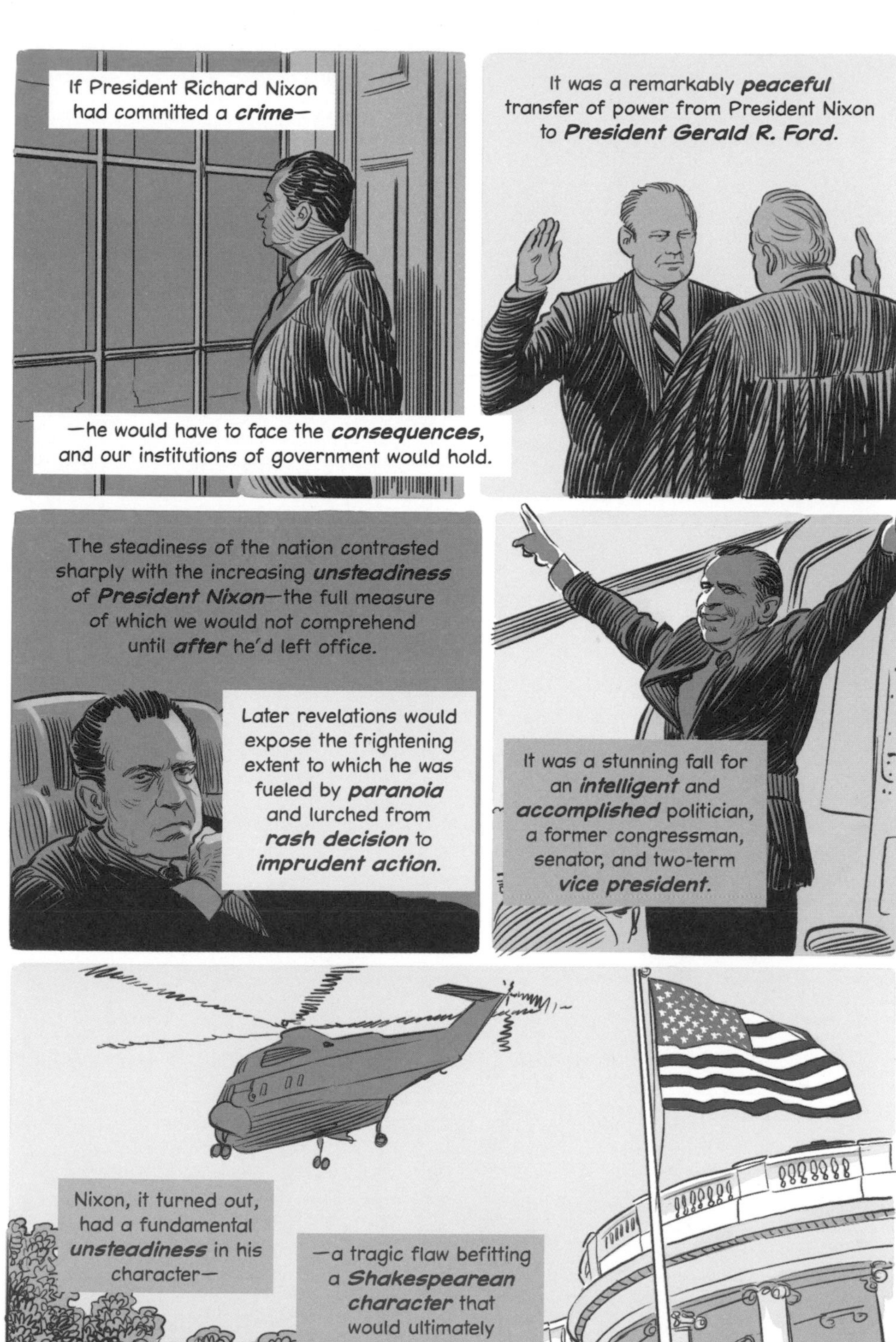
If President Richard Nixon had committed a *crime*—
—he would have to face the *consequences*, and our institutions of government would hold.
It was a remarkably *peaceful* transfer of power from President Nixon to *President Gerald R. Ford.*
The steadiness of the nation contrasted sharply with the increasing *unsteadiness* of *President Nixon*—the full measure of which we would not comprehend until *after* he'd left office.
Later revelations would expose the frightening extent to which he was fueled by *paranoia* and lurched from *rash decision* to *imprudent action.*
It was a stunning fall for an *intelligent* and *accomplished* politician, a former congressman, senator, and two-term *vice president*.
Nixon, it turned out, had a fundamental *unsteadiness* in his character—
—a tragic flaw befitting a *Shakespearean character* that would ultimately prove his *undoing.*

When a nation **sits atop** the world order—and no nation in modern history has grown to become as **powerful** as the **United States**—
—that position comes with great **responsibility**.

Yet danger lies where, as with **Watergate**, there is a **reckless** and **impetuous** hand at the helm.

While we have a reputation as a young and sometimes **brash republic**, our greatest leaders have been men and women of **prudence**, **wisdom**, and **composure**.

Our United States could never have **survived** against the incredible odds facing its birth and maturation without this sense of **equilibrium**—
—this **steadiness**.

Don't get me **wrong**.
Our nation must also embrace **volatile voices**.
Some of our greatest artists and thinkers were men and women of turbulent and **explosive** minds and temperament.

These are the cauldrons in which **new ideas** are formed.
We need to be a society that hears the sometimes uncomfortable notes of **radicalism**.

We need entrepreneurs who are willing to **risk everything** on wild dreams.
But those **risks** must not be allowed to engulf the whole in **chaos**, especially in the governance of **our country**.

It will come as no surprise to those who have worked with me that one of my favorite words is "*steady*."

It is the word I reached for when I had heard that *President Kennedy* had been shot.

It was the word that I cautioned the world to heed after the *terrorist attacks* of September 11, 2001, as we were recoiling in a state of *shock* and *horror*.
Many times I felt anxiety closing in, when my heartbeat quickened and my world began to wobble, and I repeated to myself, "*Steady*."

It is a word that I learned from my *father*, on account of it being one of his favorite words, as well.

When I was a child, I was stricken with *rheumatic fever*, and my parents feared that it would prove debilitating or even fatal.

I was confined to my bed under doctor's orders and I have distinct memories of my mother *weeping*.
I sometimes whimpered at the injustice of *my fate*, and my father would come into my room to stand over me, *lovingly but firmly*.

Steady, Danny.

Steady.

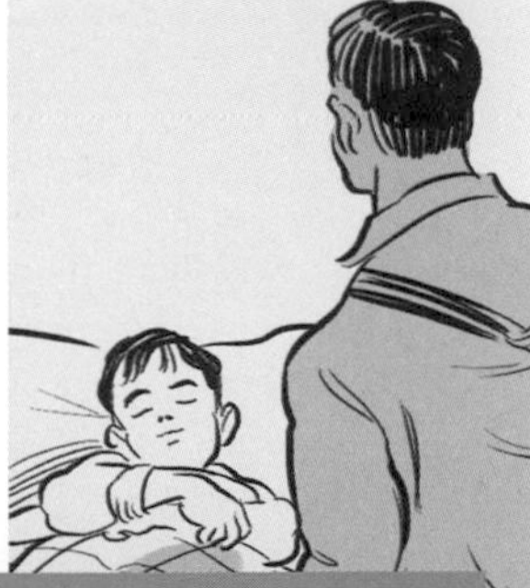
The words were clear and deliberate, and they were *soothing*. At the time, I was too young to fully absorb his *simple lesson*.

To keep me *occupied*, my parents moved a radio into my bedroom—
—and it is there that I met my *childhood hero*, the great CBS News war reporter—
—*Edward R. Murrow.*
This is *London*...
These were very *frightening times*, when it seemed that the world would succumb to the forces of *evil.*
Murrow painted the picture with *calmness* and care. He was pretty darn *steady* himself.
CBS
I listened to Murrow and many others throughout the *entire war*, as I was slowed by another bout of rheumatic fever. In the early years of the war, the news was *often grim*.
But *slowly*, the tides of war shifted.
I emerged from my illness with *no long-term consequences* to my health, and the United States emerged *victorious at war*.
I was armed with the *lesson* of my father, my hero Murrow, and *my country:*
Stay *steady*.

Even as I was **growing up** amid **turmoil**, I had a sense that a very different era had **preceded** my birth.
The ***Roaring Twenties*** were related to me in stories that seemed to be of a distant time, although they were but a ***few years earlier***.

It was nicknamed the "***decade of normalcy***" and it had been ***anything but***.
It was a time of heady, giddy ***confidence***. A ***Great War*** won (hailed at the time as *the war to end all wars*), and a stock market that ***only went up***.

And then it all ***crashed***—
WALL ST. CRASH
—leaving my parents and their generation knowing ***far too well*** the meaning of another ***important lesson*** in the human condition:
the cost of ***arrogance***.

Luckily the United States found itself under President Franklin Roosevelt—
—one of the most unwavering leaders in our history.

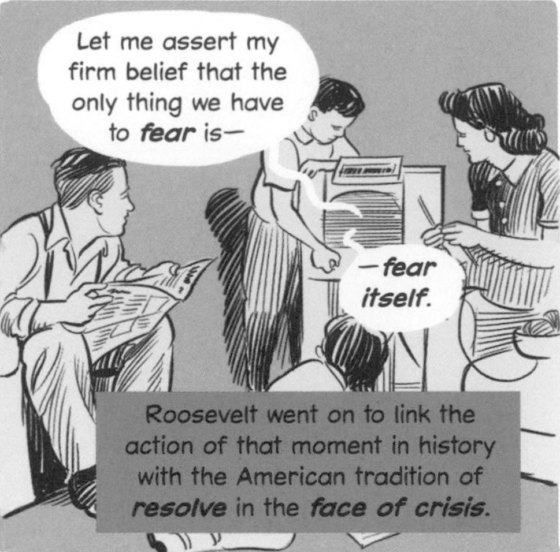
Let me assert my firm belief that the only thing we have to fear is—
—fear itself.
Roosevelt went on to link the action of that moment in history with the American tradition of resolve in the face of crisis.

Fear is a nameless, unreasoning, unjustified terror which paralyzes needed efforts to convert retreat into advance.
In every dark hour of our national life a leadership of frankness and vigor has met with that understanding and support of the people themselves which is essential to victory.

President Roosevelt's steadiness gave the nation the confidence it needed to overcome the twin challenges of economic hardship and war.

The very structure of our national government was conceived with steadiness in mind.
Our Constitution was the product of havoc that had beset the country under the weaker structure of the Articles of Confederation.

But our Founders, who had chafed under a monarchy, also worried about arrogance, and thus built a steady government with checks and balances on power to protect against
malignant recklessness.

House of Representatives

—big, boisterous, and elected frequently
—set up to channel the changing passions of the populace

President

—independently elected, but accountable to other branches

Senate

—a place of deliberation

Independent Judiciary

—able to rise above the pettiness of politics

States would serve as their own "laboratories of democracy."

It had worked ***remarkably well***, but we have sometimes, over the course of our history, lost our way into arrogance and ***unsteadiness***.

These are the ***flip sides*** of what is often referred to as ***American exceptionalism***.

It is true that we are a ***unique nation*** with a unique history.

However, that does not bestow on us a birthright of ***superiority***. When we have believed in our own invincibility, we have gotten into ***trouble***.

With the end of World War II, the national psyche of the United States brimmed with an unbridled confidence.
In that confidence were the seeds of a looming conceit.

The Korean War, the war of my young adult life—called "the forgotten war" for a reason—is one to which we should all pay closer attention.
Stuck between the glorious retellings of World War II and the contentious debate over Vietnam, the Korean conflict is often seen as tangential.
I see it as transformative—for me, personally, but also for the country because it changed the United States in fundamental ways.
Up until that point, when it came to war, America won.
We had just fought a global two-ocean conflict and vanquished our enemies.
In the years that followed, we continued to win everywhere—militarily, economically, socially, culturally. We were on a roll.
Unstoppable.
And then, suddenly, seemingly out of nowhere, came the North Korean invasion. Our allies in South Korea were driven within a hairsbreadth of being pushed off the peninsula.
The myth of American invincibility after World War II had been pierced.
The war descended into a bloody slog that ended in stalemate.
Back on the home front, much of the public was also convinced that the country was crawling with Americans spying for the Soviet Union.
It was a time of the frenzied witch hunts of McCarthyism.

When the Korean War broke out, I was a student at the tiny Sam Houston State Teachers College.
A large percentage of the male student body was either drafted or called up from the reserves.
I was not eligible for the draft on account of my rheumatic fever as a child, but I felt the deep pull of a war that seemed to be my destiny to fight.
I was able-bodied and wanted to drop out of college to head to Asia to serve under the flag of my country.
My mother would have none of it.
Since I was the first in my family to attend college, she insisted, on familial pride, that—
A Rather would finish what he started.

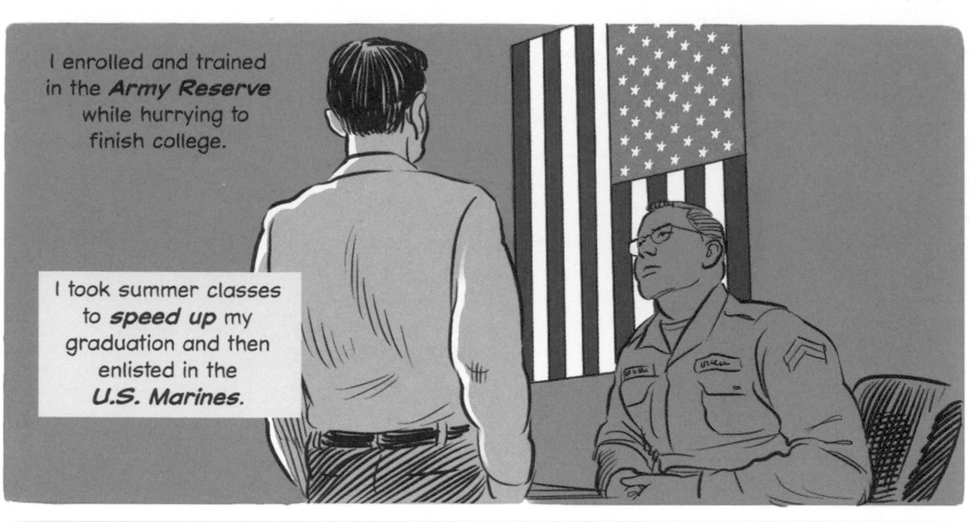
I enrolled and trained in the *Army Reserve* while hurrying to finish college.
I took summer classes to *speed up* my graduation and then enlisted in the *U.S. Marines*.

After failing to truthfully answer a question about my *childhood illness*, I was sent to *boot camp*.
I had the damn fool *idea* I was going to go in as the *lowest enlisted man* and rise to the rank of *officer*.
I dreamed of a *glorious* military career. I reported for duty in *San Diego*.

I *wince* now to think back at my exaggerated sense of *self-worth* on account of having *graduated* from *college*.
At boot camp, I was destined to crash into a *wall* of *reality*.
You are *nothing*!
You are *insignificant*!
RATHER
(Although these sentiments were usually expressed in more colorful language.)

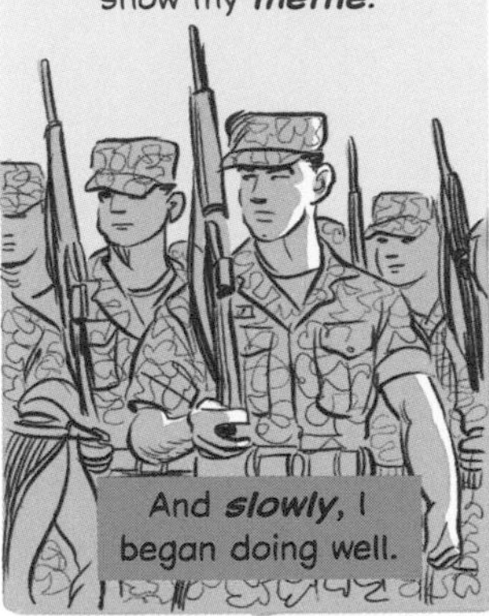
This was all much more difficult than I'd imagined, but I was determined to show my **mettle.**
And **slowly,** I began doing well.

I was sent to the Marine doctors on base for some **severe aches** in my lower extremities.
Have you ever had **rheumatic fever?**

Yes, sir. I did.
This time, I knew **better** than to lie.

He walked away without uttering another word.
I was pulled out of the ranks and sent to a "**casual company.**"

My job was to clean the noncommissioned officers' **latrine**—for days on end.

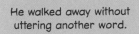

I didn't know it at the time, but the Marines had sent a **letter** to my family doctor back in Houston, **Louis Cope,** asking about my medical record.

He wrote back that I had indeed had rheumatic fever and he was **appalled** I had enlisted.

I still **have** that letter.
I was given a **medical discharge**—

—and one of the **shortest** and least distinguished careers in U.S. Marine history came to an end.

I was **humiliated** and **outraged.**
I **knew** I was fit to serve.
I would eventually see **much war** in my lifetime, far too much war.
But I saw it carrying a **reporter's notebook** instead of a rifle.

So often when you feel **most confident** and most secure, you are in the greatest **danger**.
We have never fully regained the **confidence** we felt at the end of World War II, or the unity.
Korea led to a long and arduous path of **questioning** our place in the world.
We did not **always** win wars, as we would soon have to relearn in **Vietnam**.
We could not take our destiny for granted, as we began to realize under the shadow of the **Cold War**.
There were **deep ruptures** and injustices within our nation—
—as we would see when the **national spotlight** shifted from the fissures of **McCarthyism** to the difficult struggle for **civil rights**.

Some may argue, and with merit, that ours is inherently a *conservative* system of government—
—one that *prevented* rapid progress on a host of *important issues.*
Unlike a *parliamentary* system, in which the leader of the *executive branch* derives his or her support from the legislature,

—we often have *divided* government with different political parties controlling the *presidency* and *Congress.*
This can often stymie *big actions.*
Whether one thinks that is a good thing or not, it usually *depends* on whether those in power align with *your political views.*
An oppositional Democratic Congress stopped *President George W. Bush* from privatizing Social Security.

And a Republican Congress blocked *President Barack Obama's* attempts to pass environmental legislation.
It is important to note that this *stability* of our system of government has only *intermittently* prevented progress.

But in recent years, I have worried increasingly that the mechanics of our government may be coming under a debilitating strain.
We have seen two presidential elections in a short span where the winner of the popular vote did not win the antiquated electoral college.
That is deeply troubling.
ELECT JONES
ELECT JONES
VOTE SMITH
VOTE
Far greater political retrenchment, exacerbated by gerrymandered congressional districts—
—has led to political parties in Congress voting as blocs, with far less room for compromise.
We have seen a push for far more ideological purity from our judges—
—and especially from those justices selected for the Supreme Court.
We have seen inaction on important issues even where there is large agreement among the voting public—for example, on background checks for gun purchases, criminal justice reform, and campaign financing.
I see all this, and I am worried—
—but I hear the voice of my father once more:
Steady, Danny. Steady.
I remind myself and others that we have been through big challenges in the past, that it often seems darkest in the present.
The pendulum of our great nation seems to have swung toward conceit and unsteadiness once again—
—but it is in our power to wrest it back.
Our government is there to serve us, not the other way around.

My friends, family, and colleagues will **tell** you—
—that I have **struggled**, as most of us do, to **walk the line** between confidence and conceit.
Such, I fear, is the **human condition**.
It seems that **each generation** must in some way learn its own lessons about **overreach**.

We would **do well** to study our history.
For in it lies not only evidence of **American greatness**, but also the need for **humility**.

And regardless of the invariable **ups and downs** that stretch before us in the future, I hope we can at least vow—
—to try to remain **steady**.
I would like to think that those around me would say that was **one lesson** I learned well.

One of the biggest tests to my own **personal steadiness**, and that of the nation, occurred with the assassination of **President John F. Kennedy**.
In the **chaotic hours** after I had reported on his death from Dallas, I finally found a moment to call my **wife, Jean**.

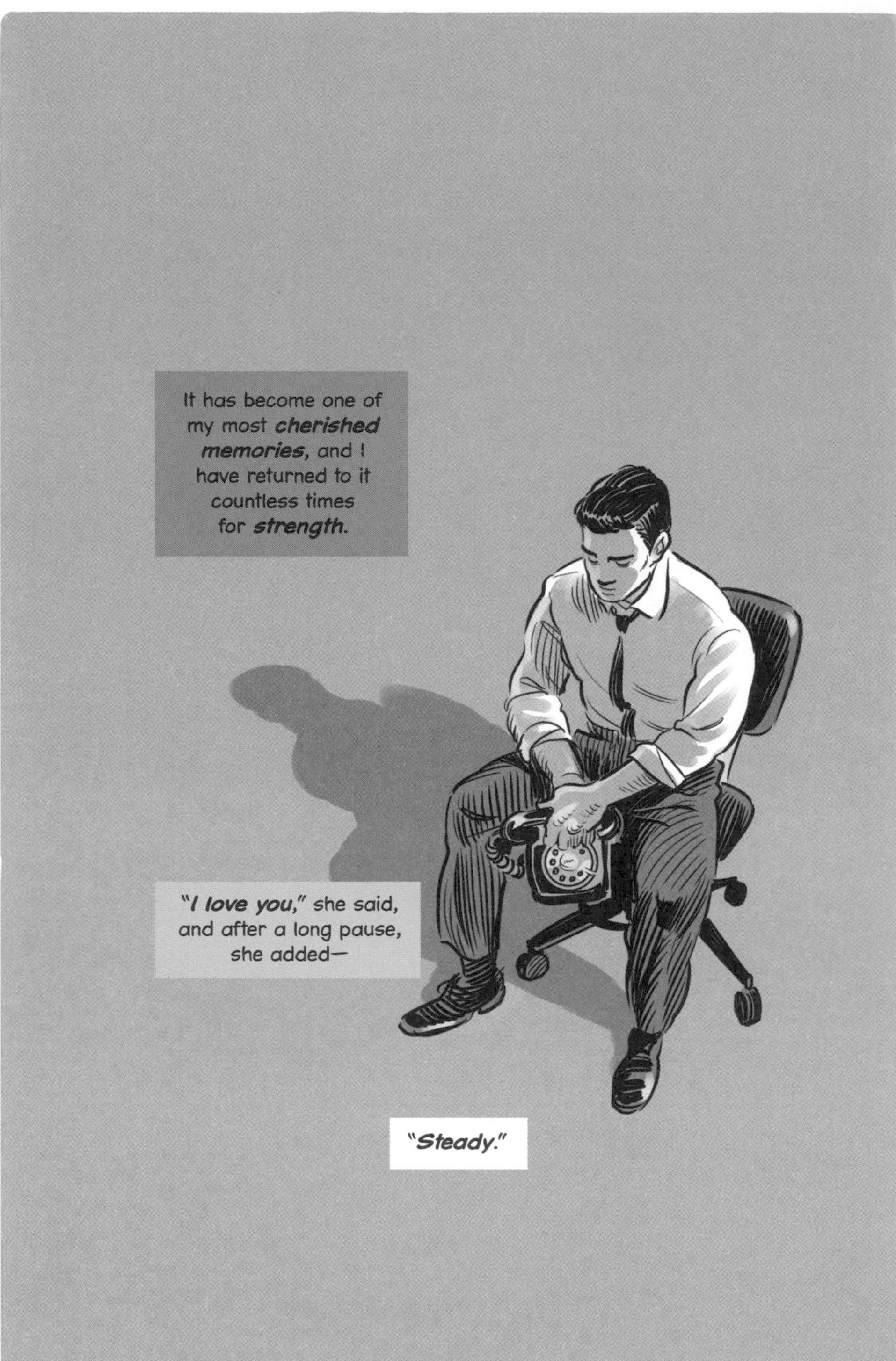
It has become one of my most *cherished memories*, and I have returned to it countless times for *strength*.
"*I love you*," she said, and after a long pause, she added—
"*Steady*."

courage
Manhattan is largely an island of straight lines—the avenues run north-south and the streets run east-west.
Having lived in New York for much of my adult life, I have grown accustomed to charting my movements according to this urban grid.
CBS BROADCAST CENTER
And for much of that time, I would undertake a daily western migration from my home on the East Side—
—to the CBS Broadcast Center, which nearly abuts the Hudson River.
This became a journey of such frequency that I knew all the landmarks on every possible route between the two points.
Time ticked onward, years into decades, but I was so rooted in my routine—
—that I felt it would go on forever, even though I knew, rationally, that all things must end.

And then suddenly it was all over.
There would be no more journeys between the two points.
A building I had entered almost as much as my own home—

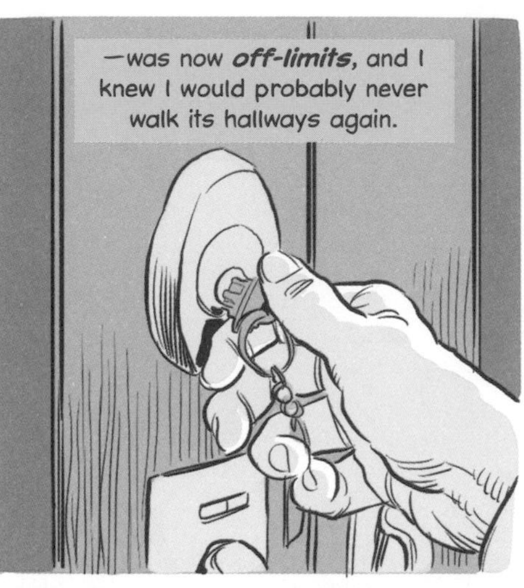
—was now off-limits, and I knew I would probably never walk its hallways again.

At first I was beset by anger—I felt I had been wronged, and I wanted answers. Few would come.
With time, my anger began to recede, and it was replaced by a sense of emptiness and sadness.

Certainties can evaporate in an instant. A life path that you expected to stretch into the future can suddenly take you off a cliff.
I knew how fortunate I was, and when I did sink into occasional periods of self-pity, Jean let me know in no uncertain terms how unattractive that quality was.

What I didn't want to admit, least of all to myself, was that I was afraid. I was afraid that this was how it was going to end, that the final chapter of my professional career had been written.

I still loved reporting and I didn't know if I was ever going to be able to do it again.

My life had been dictated for years by a sense of *order*, in a career and a place of *work*.
I could feel hints of *chaos* closing in.

When I would read the stories in the *morning papers*, I wanted to still be reporting *myself*.
I was eager for *meaningful work* and, to be completely honest, to show I still *had it*.

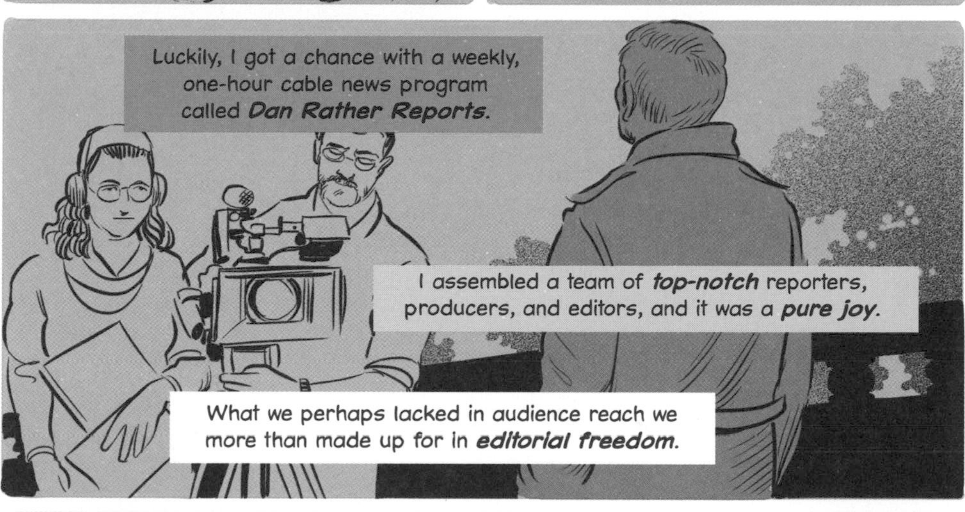
Luckily, I got a chance with a weekly, one-hour cable news program called *Dan Rather Reports*.
I assembled a team of *top-notch* reporters, producers, and editors, and it was a *pure joy*.
What we perhaps lacked in audience reach we more than made up for in *editorial freedom*.

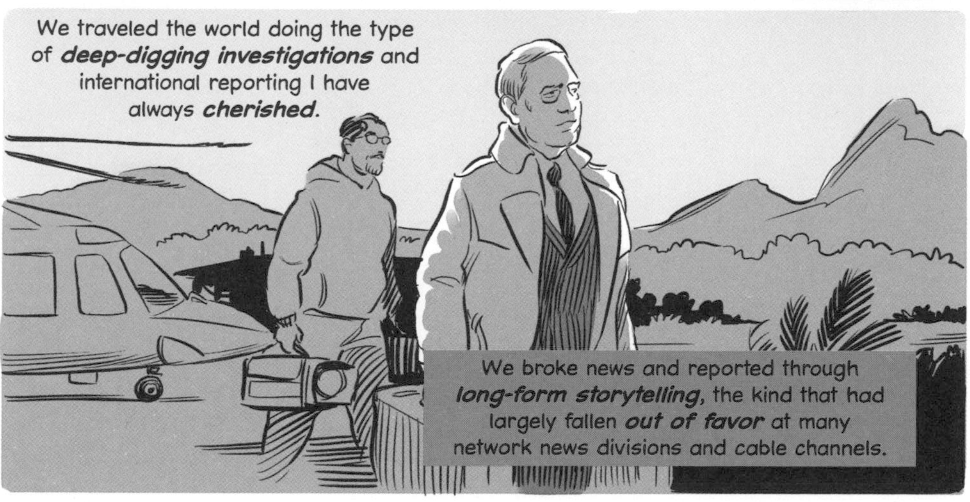
We traveled the world doing the type of *deep-digging investigations* and international reporting I have always *cherished*.
We broke news and reported through *long-form storytelling*, the kind that had largely fallen *out of favor* at many network news divisions and cable channels.

I have long lived by the precept

"Courage is being afraid, but going on anyhow."

And eventually my fear of meaninglessness after CBS News dissipated. I felt I had not only persevered—I had ***thrived.***

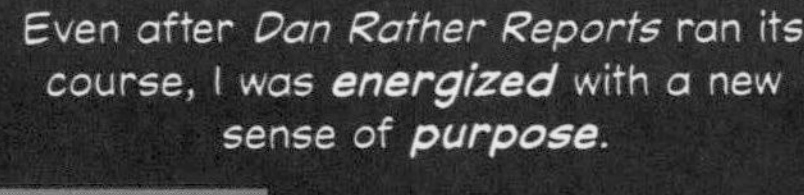
Even after *Dan Rather Reports* ran its course, I was ***energized*** with a new sense of ***purpose.***

I embraced ***social media.***
I launched a ***production company***—

—and I continue to read through several newspapers each morning looking for the next ***great story*** to chase.

Courage, I know—
—means going ***forward.***

Recently, I have thought back to my own personal journey as the nation has careened into an ***existential crisis.***
The order of the past, of how governments were meant to run and how presidents were ***supposed to behave,*** has cracked.

I ***worry*** especially for the young children.
What must they ***think*** of our perilous state?

However, it would be fatalistic to think that we are powerless.
Life is about creating order out of chaos.
In the natural world, cells come together to form complex living beings.
That's pretty orderly, and inspirational.
And we can do something similar by bringing order to our own lives for the betterment of our community.
The heroes we laud today in our history books are mostly men and women who stood up and said, "The work may be hard, the personal rewards uncertain, but we refuse to accept that the world cannot be made a better place."
The list of such people is long and wonderfully diverse.
Jane Addams
Pioneering social worker
Jackie Robinson
Integrated Major League Baseball
Cesar Chavez
Fought for rights of farmworkers
Ida B. Wells
Investigative journalist
John Muir
Naturalist and writer
Eleanor Roosevelt
Advocate for the marginalized and dispossessed
"Fighting Bob" La Follette
Campaigned against political corruption
Harvey Milk
First openly gay elected official in the United States
"The arc of the moral universe is long, but it bends toward justice."
—Dr. Martin Luther King Jr.

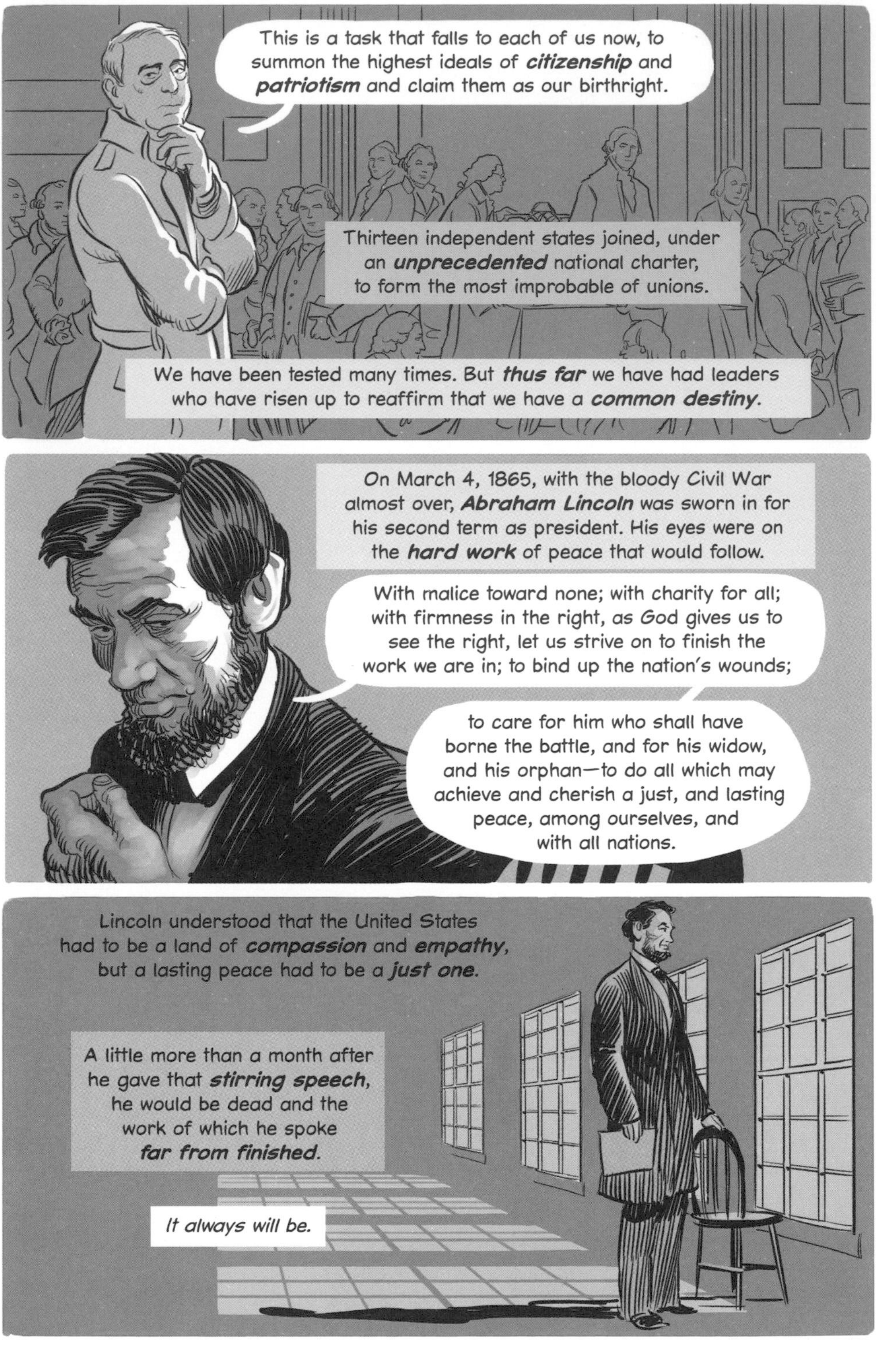

This is a task that falls to each of us now, to summon the highest ideals of ***citizenship*** and ***patriotism*** and claim them as our birthright.

Thirteen independent states joined, under an ***unprecedented*** national charter, to form the most improbable of unions.

We have been tested many times. But ***thus far*** we have had leaders who have risen up to reaffirm that we have a ***common destiny***.

On March 4, 1865, with the bloody Civil War almost over, ***Abraham Lincoln*** was sworn in for his second term as president. His eyes were on the ***hard work*** of peace that would follow.

With malice toward none; with charity for all; with firmness in the right, as God gives us to see the right, let us strive on to finish the work we are in; to bind up the nation's wounds;

to care for him who shall have borne the battle, and for his widow, and his orphan—to do all which may achieve and cherish a just, and lasting peace, among ourselves, and with all nations.

Lincoln understood that the United States had to be a land of ***compassion*** and ***empathy***, but a lasting peace had to be a ***just one***.
A little more than a month after he gave that ***stirring speech***, he would be dead and the work of which he spoke ***far from finished***.
It always will be.

As we seek **common ground** with our fellow citizens, we cannot **forsake** our core values.
Compromise cannot be confused with **capitulation**.

Recently, **many** of you have come up to me and **asked:**
What can or should I do in a country I no longer seem to **recognize**?

Ultimately, democracy is an **action** more than a belief.
The people's voice, **your voice**, must be heard for it to have an effect.

Currently, many **hurdles** diminish the power of our **collective speech**, such as how we finance campaigns, our discriminatory voting laws, and the preferred place of moneyed interests in Washington.

Despite all these **obstacles**, I am enough of an optimist to believe that if we **come together** to speak, and vote, and participate, the nation will bend its path.

It is especially important that we engage in action for our **children**.

This struggle is not only about creating the country we wish them to inherit, it is also about **teaching them**
(and re-learning ourselves)
how democracy is **rooted** in civic activity.

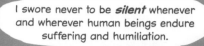

Holocaust survivor **Elie Wiesel,** in his acceptance speech for the **Nobel Peace Prize,** said:

I swore never to be silent whenever and wherever human beings endure suffering and humiliation.
We must always take sides.
Neutrality helps the oppressor, never the victim. Silence encourages the tormentor, never the tormented.
Sometimes we must interfere.

I always stood in awe of his positive but determined approach to life, this from a man who had lost his parents and sister to the concentration camps.

It is sometimes easy to magnify one's own struggles or the difficulties of the present age.

In the face of people like Wiesel, or those who are confronting serious illness or economic hardship,
I marvel anew at the resilience of the human spirit.

I understand that my time to ***shape*** and ***help*** this world is passing.
This is the circle of ***life.***
I hope now to ***inspire others*** to love this country, to pledge to ***work hard*** to make it a healthier and more ***just*** place to live.
I ultimately have faith in the ***basic decency*** of our American citizenry, and indeed people around the globe.
I believe strongly that the ***core tenets*** I love most about this nation can be a foundation for ***commonality*** and ***strength*** once more.

I believe in a wide and expansive *vision* of our national destiny.
And I believe in *all of you* to help make it a reality.
Courage.

afterword

SAVE

In the aftermath of one of the most divisive elections in American history, when so many were calculating all that was wrong with our national moment, we sought to write a book about core values that could serve as a foundation for reconciliation.

We saw *What Unites Us* as a statement of our democratic ideals. But as I traveled across the country over the past two years, I learned that the title of our book had become an urgent question: What unites us? Many of you asked this question with tears in your eyes and a quiver in your voice, reflecting all that you feared had already been lost. You pointed to deep fissures over race, religion, culture, geography, and even decency. You asked whether the great American experiment was doomed, whether we'd be torn apart by division and disunion. Had we forgotten about what unites us? Or was it always just a mirage?

It is only natural to wonder whether our future will be defined more by dire questions and conflict than by shared values. Undoubtedly, it will be some combination of the two. And as I hope you discovered in reading this book, it has always been thus in the American story. The chief variable is inevitably one of balance: Will instability overwhelm all that we have established? Or will we unite enough to tackle our challenges?

Much has been written about how tribal we are getting. We see it in our social media feeds, and it is reflected in the increased polarization of our political parties along geographic and social divisions. But I do not believe we will be perpetually and hopelessly divided along the boundaries we now see. I have lived long enough to see healing where there was once hatred. I remember the horrors of World War II and have since traveled many times to Germany, Japan, and Italy to report on their place as strong allies of the United States. I have seen bigots turned into champions for civil rights. Despite some governmental and judicial intransigence, I have seen a sweeping change in acceptance by families and society at large for members of the LGBTQ community. And there are many other reasons for hope. I have seen that minds can be changed and believe a national healing can take place, despite real impediments in our voting process, despite the dissemination of news and propaganda. There is still a place for optimism, but only if it is bolstered by hard work, perseverance, and a commitment by each of us to improve the well-being of our communities.

When I say some version of this in public, I am often met by another set of questions from many of you who say you desperately want to believe in a better future. So many people are eager for a blueprint for action, a checklist for how to defend our democracy. You ask, "What can I do to save my country?"

Through a career in journalism, I have learned that there are no easy answers or fail-proof plans of action. But since our system of government is one of representative democracy, the power of the vote must be paramount. And with recent elections we have seen the importance of enfranchisement reaffirmed. Essential to change is making sure that you vote, and get others to do so. To amplify the vote, we must also volunteer in political movements, knock on doors, encourage and enable others to join in the electoral process. I have been heartened by a swelling of such activism: from women's marches to protests organized by teenagers, so many fearless people have come forward, buoyed by the strength that comes from fighting for their beliefs and joining a cause greater than their own circle of existence.

This spirit was evident in the wake of the mass shooting at Marjory Stoneman Douglas High School in Parkland, Florida. Initially, many of us had the sickening feeling that another senseless tragedy would be devoured by cynicism, with no change to the political stasis around gun violence. But many of the students, fueled

GET
INVOLVED!
BE
HEARD

by an understandable anger, vowed action—and a movement began. I was able to interview several of the newly minted activists a few months after the tragedy and I was inspired by what I heard and saw. Despite the horror they had lived through, these young Americans expressed the idealism that serves as one of youth's most endearing qualities. As the next election season approached, they directed their energy to political engagement. They understood not only the power of the vote but also the commitment it takes to organize and keep momentum going. And they were matched by other groups, female and minority voters, who threw themselves into the business of political activism, all of which resulted in record turnout for our midterm elections and new movement on gun legislation.

But while politics is of central importance, the effort to improve the health of our nation must be infused into all aspects of life, and it must be an obligation that each of us feels is part of our daily duty to our nation. I hope we can realize the power that each individual citizen possesses, and in so doing, what can and should unite us.

Now that I am at an age where the circle of life is never far from my mind, I increasingly turn to some of my earliest memories to help steady my thoughts. The obligations and opportunities that come with being a citizen of this country were a consistent presence of my youth. I can still remember clearly the run-down building on Shepherd Drive that served as the local civic club in our Houston neighborhood. In addition to a space for celebrations like weddings, it was also a gathering place for political meetings and discussions of the needs of the community. I can recall a passionate discussion about efforts to petition the city to lay down gravel on what was still a dirt street nearby. Above all, I remember the spirit that building embodied. It provided a forum for people to make their voices heard. I remember the faces of the men and women as they talked over matters big and small in their lives, how they might engage with their government and how their government should engage with them. I remember the sense of community, that we all had a role to play in making our country function properly.

These early instincts were cultivated in seventh grade when we were required to take a class in civics. We learned about the branches of government and the divisions between federal, state, and local jurisdictions. We learned about the difference between mayors and city managers.

And we learned how bills become laws. I remember much of the focus was on how the city of Houston worked, and that an actual city government official visited our class. The lesson was meant to be clear: this was our city, and by extension our state and our country. That sense of ownership came with both duty and opportunity. Unfortunately, what we were not taught was that in other parts of the city, young boys and girls were segregated at separate and unequal schools, and they were learning very different lessons about whether this country was for them. The chasm over race and citizenship is inescapable in American history, and it casts a shadow over almost every conceivable aspect of our national story.

I would learn about these injustices later in life, and I believe that my own knowledge of civics, though idealized, prepared me to grapple with its failures in the United States as well as celebrate its successes. Civics was one of my favorite classes in school because it felt like one of the "Code-O-Graph" decoders we got for the old Captain Midnight radio show. It was a way of deciphering what was going on in the world around us. It was a means to determine who had power, and why. And it was a guide for understanding the distance between reality and the ideals of the nation embodied in our sacred founding documents.

Still, it stuck with me that in our working-class school, in what we may now call a marginal neighborhood, there was an expectation that we understand how our country worked. We had a role to play in the governance of America every bit as much as the wealthy people in town. It may sound corny, but I think civics can be one of the most empowering things we can teach our children. It tells them that this nation belongs to them, all of them.

CIVICS

Civics classes fell out of favor for many decades, and not surprisingly, studies have shown that basic awareness of the mechanics of our government is perilously low. I am heartened to see civics making a bit of a comeback, at least anecdotally. When it is not taught, our young people learn that they don't have to worry about government, that they can leave it to others: the rich, the well connected, the ones who've lived in this country longer, or their elders. How do we expect people to participate in something they don't understand? And when we teach civics, it shouldn't be from textbooks only. Civics is about action, about dealing with and trying to improve the present. Students need to hear from elected officials and government workers who look and talk like them. They need to see that it is their right to walk the corridors of power, that they are very much the "average American citizen" as anyone else.

Through the nature of my work, I have interviewed presidents and queens, billionaires and generals, sports legends and movie moguls. In history textbooks, these often are the men and women mentioned in bold. They are the "important people," the heroes (and sometimes villains) who shape the destiny of the rest of us. But I have learned that this isn't really how the world works. I have met countless others over the years whose names will never be known beyond a small circle of family and friends but whose actions change lives. And time and again I have seen how individual voices can swell into waves that have the power to shift the course of history, such as the growing number of women and minorities elected to office. This is how, in the face of great hurdles and inequality, we can turn "what unites us" from a question into an answer.

Perhaps the path to what unites us could be paved with a recommitment to citizenship. I recognize that the very idea of citizenship has become a point of contention in our current environment, as it has been for much of American history. But like the idea of patriotism, I will not surrender the word "citizenship" to those who use it as a tool for disenfranchisement and division or who wish to return us to a mythic past when the rights of citizenship were unevenly granted.

Our times require a modern sense of citizenship. Citizenship is not merely a collection of conferred rights but a compact with each other to work for the well-being of all, to engage with our civic institutions, to support our schools, the democratic process, and the health of our environment. It must be based on more than the

geographic accident of one's birth. Being a citizen of the United States confers a great set of advantages about which we should feel humble. I seek a sense of citizenship that transcends geography, gender, class, race, religion, and sexual orientation. It must be as open to the newest additions to our American family as it is to those whose family tree was planted here generations ago.

Furthermore, citizenship cannot be passive. We have seen the danger of believing that the country will just take care of itself. For years I observed a level of complacency; America's changing demographics, it was thought, would put the nation on a predetermined path of progress and greater inclusivity. Our

VOTE

institutions of civil government and democratic norms, buttressed by our constitutional protections, were largely assumed to be too strong to be damaged in any meaningful way by the winds of popular sentiment. Some warned that powerful political actors—abetted by structural impediments in our electoral system—were working to undermine our democratic freedoms. This was a cause for concern. But few, including myself, believed that these reactionist forces could infiltrate our national consciousness and threaten what were once assumed to be our unassailable values. But that is exactly what they have done, and they have done so with the encouragement of millions of vocal supporters.

There has been, among many, a palpable and understandable fear that the country is lost. I took a call on my radio program shortly after election day in 2016 from a distraught young woman who had been planning to get married, buy a house, and start a family. She wondered whether she should still pursue those dreams. Would she have to leave the United States? I could hear pain and fear in her voice. And it struck me deeply that someone so young, with so much of life ahead of her, could feel so lost and scared. I tried to counsel her not to give up on herself or her country. I told her I believed things would be okay, but of course, whether in our personal lives or the larger scope of our country, one never fully knows. We can't afford to be Pollyannas or blind ourselves to real dangers, but we also should try not to succumb to despair. If we believe our vision for what our country is is worth fighting for, then we should fight for it. This is our right and duty as citizens.

I have an unshakable belief in the basic goodness of the vast majority of the American people, and I felt, in the wake of the 2016 election, that my fellow citizens would rise to this challenge, as well. Indeed, we have witnessed a groundswell of engagement and momentum in pushing back against the forces of intolerance

RELIEF

and fighting for what President Lincoln once called "the better angels of our nature." I wonder: Can the notion of citizenship be infused with not only activism, but heroism, as well? I'm thinking of the definition of heroism as outlined by one of the great thinkers of the American journey, the philosopher Ralph Waldo Emerson. In his essay "Heroism," he makes a bold and compassionate plea for the power of individual action in service of helping others and promoting truth. And he also calls for sustained action. "The characteristic of heroism is its persistency," he wrote. And he acknowledges that many heroic actions go without notice. “Do not take back your words when you find that prudent people do not commend you. Adhere to your own act, and congratulate yourself if you have done something strange and extravagant, and broken the monotony of a decorous age.” And he noted, rightly, that “times of heroism are generally times of terror, but the day never shines in which this element may not work.” We often like to think of heroes as others. On reporting trips to natural disasters or other sites of terror or tragedy, I can’t tell you how often I heard the phrase “I am no hero” from someone who had performed heroically. If we can elevate and share this idea of personal heroism, I believe we will be on the path to mending our republic.

I do not see this search for heroic citizenship as a quixotic quest. We are a can-do people. There’s a story I once heard that captures this spirit with the elegance of an ancient parable. The setting was Germany during World War II and the narrator was a young woman, in her teens at the time. She witnessed the German army up close and saw that when the tanks broke down or got stuck, the soldiers would wait around for an officer to tell them what to do. But when the American GIs rolled in, she was struck by the difference. Their tanks invariably also broke down and got stuck, but there was no waiting around. Soldiers would jump out and immediately go to work trying to fix things themselves. They worked together and they were completely self-motivated. That is the American

spirit I have seen echoed time and again, in datelines too numerous to count.

This is the embodiment of heroic citizenship, a commitment to each other and to fixing problems. It is seeking solutions and not praise, progress and not personal aggrandizement.

It is doing what is right for the sake of right. I have seen this spirit as a common denominator that cuts across all aspects of American society. I have seen it on distant and dangerous battlefields, and in the wake of natural disasters. I have seen it recently in children advocating for action on climate change and teachers working to confront bullying. I have seen it in those volunteering to help the homeless and those providing compassion to opioid addicts. None of us is perfect, and we all have our lesser moments. There are many people whose hearts are infected with hatred, bigotry, and selfishness. But I firmly believe that they are a distinct minority and that we can all summon up our better qualities to help improve this nation.

When Hurricane Harvey struck my hometown of Houston in the summer of 2017, help came pouring in from all directions. Many who volunteered to save lives were not even legal citizens of the United States. In a Texas that was riven like much of the country over the immigration debate, no one was asking if the people manning the boats that came to save them had their legal papers. The idea of heroic citizenship is even bigger than legal citizenship itself. But as the crisis passed, so, too, did some (but thankfully not all) of the collective spirit. How can we keep these bonds strong and how can we extend them to beyond our immediate neighbors? Shortly after Harvey struck Texas, Hurricanes Irma and Maria struck the U.S. Virgin Islands and Puerto Rico. There the response from our government for our fellow citizens was completely inadequate. The tragedy confirmed deep strains of disunity. How could we have let our people down so badly? There was outrage, but our government didn't respond with nearly the urgency or empathy needed. And the resulting pain and death will always be a cause for national regret. Once again comes the haunting question: What unites us?

DAN
RATHER
WHAT
UNITES
US

My deepest concern is that we lose a sense of a common national community, that we retrench into like-minded enclaves where we look out for ourselves and the people like us. The values I have sought to explore in this book are ones that can and should transcend these divisions. But we have seen that they cannot be taken for granted, that they need that energy of heroic citizenship.

Ultimately, heroic citizenship must be rooted in the possible. And that means it must manifest itself in almost infinite forms of expression. None of us is alike. We all have our strengths and weaknesses, and ultimately it is that diversity that provides the strongest glue that can hold this nation together. My hope is that you have seen your own actions and strengths or the actions of people you know celebrated in some of the essays here. For whether we are artists, scientists, soldiers, journalists, teachers, caregivers, nurses, farmers, mechanics, foster parents, friends in times of need, or really anyone who puts energy, heart, and mind into helping others, we have within ourselves the power to be heroic in service to our country. And by doing so, we will help answer the question of what unites us.

UAW
STRIKE
UAW
LOCAL
STRIKE

acknowledgments

It is customary in the acknowledgments to recognize that a book often represents a labor of love, and the tendrils of its creation extend far beyond the names on the cover. That is especially true of *What Unites Us*, which started as a written narrative and now has been transformed into this spectacularly visual creation. The credit for this new edition goes to the incredibly talented artist Tim Foley; to Mark Siegel, Robyn Chapman, Kirk Benshoff, and Sunny Lee of First Second, who somehow saw in our original words the potential for this new manifestation; and to the incisive editing of Sara Rosenbaum. To them, and all the others who worked on this project, we owe a debt of gratitude and no small amount of wonder. This new creation couldn't have been done without the original, and we renew our thanks to our friends, family, and colleagues, and the team at Algonquin who supported, urged, and consoled us through that creative process.

Most of all, however, we would like to thank all of you who renew our faith in this country and its people every day. This nation has, and always will be, a work in progress. It may be blessed with abundant natural resources, but its greatest gifts have been its lofty ideals and the people who work to make them more of a reality. We wrote this book not as a lecture. Rather, we hoped it would inspire dialogues across the many divides of our nation. And we are excited that in its new form it may find its way into the hands of different types of readers. So thank you for giving it a try, and we hope you are encouraged to add your voice to the American story.

—Dan Rather and Elliot Kirschner

Dan Rather is one of the world's best-known journalists, with a storied career that has spanned more than six decades. He has interviewed every president since Eisenhower and covered almost every important dateline around the world. Rather joined CBS News in 1962, and in 1981 he assumed the position of anchor and managing editor of the *CBS Evening News,* which he held for twenty-four years. His reporting helped turn *60 Minutes* into an institution, launched *48 Hours* as a newsmagazine program, and shaped countless specials and documentaries. Upon leaving CBS, Rather created the Emmy Award–winning *Dan Rather Reports* on HDNet. He is founder, president, and CEO of News and Guts, an independent production company that specializes in high-quality nonfiction content across a range of traditional and digital channels.

Elliot Kirschner is a *New York Times* bestselling author and Emmy Award–winning news producer and documentary filmmaker. Growing up, he was captivated by his grandparents recounting a world very different from his own. After studying American history and literature at Harvard, he spent nearly twenty years in New York City, where he began his long collaboration with Dan Rather. He cofounded the Wonder Collaborative, an experiment in science filmmaking in his native San Francisco, where he lives with his wife, Malia, and daughters, Eva and Helena, who think he tells the best bedtime stories.

Tim Foley was born in Flint, Michigan, and since attending college at the Kendall School of Design, has made his home in Grand Rapids on the west side of the state. A freelance illustrator for the past three decades, his work has appeared in magazines and newspapers around the world, and his books have included many titles in the bestselling young adult Who Was biography series, as well as several adult coloring books.

:01
First Second

Published by arrangement with Algonquin Books
This book is a graphic novel adaptation of the nonfiction book
What Unites Us: Reflections on Patriotism, which was originally published in 2017
by Algonquin Books of Chapel Hill, a division of Workman Publishing Co., Inc.

Published by First Second
First Second is an imprint of Roaring Brook Press,
a division of Holtzbrinck Publishing Holdings Limited Partnership
120 Broadway, New York, NY 10271

Library of Congress Control Number: 2020911200
ISBN: 978-1-250-23994-5

First graphic novel edition, 2021

FIRST
EDITION

Graphic novel edition edited by Mark Siegel, Whit Taylor, and S. I. Rosenbaum
Cover design by Kirk Benshoff
Interior book design by Sunny Lee

Printed in Singapore

Artwork created digitally with a Wacom tablet and Corel Painter software
(using the cover pencil tool for pencils and layouts and the scratchboard tool for the inks).
Lettering and layer compiling done in Photoshop.

1 3 5 7 9 10 8 6 4 2

BY ART
WE LIVE